Thailand

An Insider's Guide for the Savvy Traveler

Dave Dunne

Table of Contents

Preface

The Land of Smiles. The Kingdom of Siam. A magical place where you can find anything and lose everything. When I stop to really think about what it is that draws people to Thailand, I can't find an answer. You can't put it into words, you just have to experience it.

And experience you shall. But you should not fall victim to the MANY pitfalls, traps and waste precious time figuring things out that you could have avoided. There are plenty of reasons why you need this guide.

The *40 Minute Travel Guide*™ series was inspired by my desire to share my insights and lessons learned during my many travels and time spent living in various countries around Asia. This is not a thorough guide book, nor is it a history lesson. You will not find detailed tours, lists of hotels or maps in this book. What you WILL find is all you need to know to make your trip much smoother than it would be, had you not read this book.

This book is designed to be read in around 40 minutes, give or take, depending on your reading speed. The reason for this is simple: That's all the time you need to effectively absorb the "to-the-point" and "must-know" insider information in this book. I will provide you with the type of information that will allow you to understand the people, avoid trouble and have a much better time than you would have had you NOT read the book. I will also provide as many links as possible to further reading on certain subjects, as well as just a few of my recommended tours, hotels and other items that may make your trip just a bit more enjoyable.

I highly recommend picking up the eBook version of this book to take advantage of the numerous useful links and maps provided. Alternatively, you should visit *www.40MinuteTravelGuru.com*. There you'll find even more material, articles and even maps of highly recommended things to do to aid you along your way, both during your trip to Thailand and many other countries.

Safe travels!

Introduction

"It's bad manners to keep Thailand waiting."

-Unknown

If you've bought this book, odds are that you're going to Thailand, or are considering doing so. Good move. Having spent a great amount of time there over the years, and even gaining some family along the way, I can say without a doubt that it's a country I know well and enjoy beyond words. Between the mysterious and wonderful culture, the amazing food and beautiful scenery to the fun-loving and kind people, it's a place that will leave you planning your next trip as soon as you leave.

In general, Thailand is a safe place, for most logical people. Crime is not rampant, and you're not very likely to be randomly assaulted or robbed. The society as a whole loves to keep their visitors entertained and safe. In fact, their economy is somewhat dependent on you having a great time and coming back. For these reasons, the focus of this book will be on:

- Understanding the culture and how to navigate it;

- Tips for getting around without problems;

- Where to go and what to do;

- Everyday must-knows, tips and tricks;

- How to enjoy your time in the smoothest and most problem-free way possible; and

- Avoiding tourist pitfalls and legal trouble.

To truly understand Thailand and the Thai people, we must first look at a brief history of Thailand leading up to the modern day, and how this history has shaped the country and its' relationships with the outside world, specifically with tourism.

Transformation into a Modern-Day Tourism Destination

From the Kingdom of Siam to The Land of Smiles

The history of Thailand (and all of Southeast Asia) is a very complex, very long and very interesting one. Originating in China, the ethnic *Tai* people migrated to modern-day Thailand around 1,000 years ago when the area was under the control of the Khmer Empire (ethnic Khmer people speaking the Khmer dialect live predominantly in northern Thailand, Laos and Cambodia currently). As the Khmer Empire weakened, the various Tai city-states went through periods of infighting until the Ayutthaya Kingdom was established, the predecessor to the Kingdom of Siam. Ayutthaya experienced a long period of war with neighboring Burma (now Myanmar) during which time the capital of Ayutthaya was burned to the ground. Out of this rose the Kingdom of Siam, later to be named Thailand, of which the current Monarchy rules to this day.

During the European colonialization periods, Siam was never colonized like Burma (English), Vietnam and Cambodia (French), its immediate neighbors. As a matter of fact, it was the only country in Southeast Asia not colonized by an outside power and instead served as a "buffer" between British and French controlled Burma and Cambodia. This lack of outside influence and control in its history is a key factor in understanding modern thinking by many Thais and the relationships it has with its neighbors. With the outbreak of World War 2, the Thai government, after being invaded, allied itself with the Japanese, more as forced neutrality than a direct alliance, allowing the Japanese to invade neighboring Burma from its borders (the term "karma" must have come to mind for some). After the war, (then named) Siam allied itself with the US, including during the Vietnam War, an alliance still in place to this day. As history has shown, Thailand maintains a headstrong approach to outside influence and it could easily be argued that allies are formed solely on the basis of perceived instant gratification and immediate benefits to Thailand over any other factor.

Naturally then, it was during the years of the US-Vietnam War that Thailand began to morph from a relatively agrarian society not much different than its neighbors to a tourism hot spot which placed it on the map as one of the top tourist destinations in the world. As a home for many US Air Bases and a popular R&R destination for the hundreds of thousands of soldiers rotating through Vietnam, the word about this magical place with its idyllic beaches, great weather, cheap prices, golden temples and beautiful people quickly spread. Sleepy fishing villages quickly began turning into resort towns. Entertainment districts sprung up

in Bangkok. A new economy began gaining steam and once the Thais

discovered money, the rest is history.

Thai Culture

Thailand is, at its core, a Buddhist country. Buddhism more or less defines the culture and day to day life in the Land of Smiles (LOS). All of the basic principles of Buddhism are at play in Thai business, family, relationships and every other facet of life. The Buddhist and cultural ideals present in daily Thai life are why the Thai people *generally* appear and act at peace with whatever may come their way. This *no worries* mindset is part of the appeal the country has for many visitors.

With that said, these same cultural ideals that bring inner Thais peace, also have the propensity to create a great amount of confusion and frustration for long time expats and tourists alike, who don't take the time to understand WHY things are the way they are and fail to adapt to the environment accordingly. Understanding the Thai culture and how to navigate it is ***absolutely*** crucial to enjoying your time in the Land of Smiles if you have any desire to maintain your sanity, of course.

Greetings

Probably the first thing you'll encounter when you arrive is the way Thais greet people, with hands pressed together, fingers touched at the top and a slight bow. This is called a *Wai*, the official greeting of Thailand.

The Wai is initiated by the younger or lower status person, meaning that it would be expected for the hotel staff to Wai you, not the other way around. You would respond with the same of course, though not doing so wouldn't be considered hugely offensive. What *would* be considered offensive is if you failed to Wai someone of a higher social status than you, perhaps if you were employed by a company in Thailand and failed to Wai the Thai CEO. As a rule of thumb, the higher the hands are in relation to the head, the more respect is being shown, an example being that you will see children Wai people with their hands clear above their head. As a tourist though, you are not expected to know these types of things and will be forgiven as such if you don't.

Tip: Take note of how Thais Wai each other. It may be useful to know who is high up on the social ladder in certain situations.

Social Status

Which brings me to my next topic: Social status is important in Thailand. Thais tend to interact with one another based on their rank on the social ladder, which determines who their friends are and the types of places they frequent. When going out, it is customary for the oldest or highest-earning member (usually the same) to pick up the tab, as doing so is a form of impressing their peers and subordinates. This is regularly confused by foreigners as stinginess when they find themselves always footing the bill when, in the Thai reality, they are consistently the highest-ranking member in the company they are keeping.

Thais can also be *very* superficial. For example, a Thai will have you sized up by country, income, and value to them within 1 second based only on your attire. So if you don't want to be the target of scams and street peddlers, don't wear a suit to go for a walk. Likewise, if you want to be taken seriously, don't wear shorts, sandals and a cut-off shirt to a nice place for the night. In the latter example, (and beyond the fact that you may not be let in the door) in the mind of Thais, this is veering way out of your social lane. In Thailand, people generally know their place on the pecking order of things and stay there. This is not to say that there is no social mobility at all, because there certainly is. It's just that Thais typically go with the flow and don't like to create waves.

For instance, you won't see a taxi driver try to gain entry to an exclusive club or dine at a nice restaurant, even if he can afford it. Doing so would simply disrupt the natural order of things. And he and all other Thais are always aware of the order of things. Wandering out of ones' social lane is a great way for a Thai to lose face.

Face/ Respect

To be clear up front: ***Never cause a Thai to lose face*** in front of other Thais. A public slight, loss of respect or humiliation means much more to a Thai than to a Westerner. The difference in definition of this concept, between your country and Thailand, is what's important to be aware of. Of course, nobody wants to be humiliated but simply put: something that would not offend someone in the West may provoke a Thai into an uncontrolled rage or otherwise create a volatile situation.

It's important to know the thresholds for what *will* and *will not* cause a Thai to lose face, as well as maintain awareness so that you can quickly steer the situation to avoid a face-loss from occurring. As friendly as those smiles are, Thais have a shocking propensity for violence, and a loss of face is the #1 trigger for it.

This may be a good place to stress that by "high propensity for violence" I do not mean a simple fist fight. I mean bottles, cutlery and hit men on motorcycles.

To be as clear as possible, below are a few scenarios where I have personally witnessed the subject Thai become irately violent. You'll likely agree that it would be a rare case for a Westerner to resort to a comparable level of violence for the same offense:

1. A taxi driver being shamed when he is lost or doesn't know how to get to a destination;

2. Showing criticism of someone's food at a food vendor stall;

3. A woman being teased for wearing cheap looking clothing;

4. A street vendor being criticized for the quality of her goods; and

5. A Thai man being disrespected by a woman choosing another man.

All are common in most cultures, not all would end in bloodshed. That's the point I am making. It's important to know the difference and always be aware of the situation. When you sense that you or someone you're with may be creating a stir, however, you can easily steer the situation with a bit of cultural finesse by restoring respect to the offended party.

Thais rarely fight one on one (except in the Muay Thai ring), especially if a foreigner is involved with another Thai.

Don't Mess with People

You get what you give. As is the case in most Asian countries, respect is reciprocated. If you are courteous and respectful to the people you meet, you will get the same. If you are a jerk, you will probably not fare well. Don't be a jerk. Thai people generally let foreigners get away with much more than they should, as long as the money is flowing, but don't push it. This is the most important thing you should know before visiting Thailand with regards to your safety. For the most part, you're pretty safe in Thailand unless you give someone a reason to wish you harm. And when that happens (and it can happen quickly) you're in for a bad day.

Smiles and *Mai Pen Rai* (No Worries/ No Problem)

As quickly as Thais can become upset, they can just as quickly forget about it and go back to life if balance is restored…usually. Thais try to not let the burdens of life upset them too much. As the nickname may suggest, in the Land of Smiles, people like to wear a smile. This is a way of keeping your troubles to yourself and making those around you feel relaxed. Smiling is also one way to let those around you know that you're not upset and everything is all good. Since we've just discussed some potentially dangerous situations, it's worth mentioning that smiling is one of the ingredients required to diffuse a volatile situation.

Mai Pen Rai indirectly translates to *"no problem/ everything is okay/ no worries"* or something similar. Ask 20 Thais and you'll get 20 different but similar definitions (different but same same? For those that get the joke). The point is, this saying makes Thais feel at ease. If a Thai feels they have let you down, or if you've maybe upset someone (or inadvertently made someone lose face), this saying, when combined with a Wai and a smile, will diffuse the situation and bring everything back to center. Take it from someone who's been inadvertently party to a few volatile situations over the years, it works like a charm.

Reverence for Royal and Religious Figures

Though the form of government is officially and functionally a Democracy, it is more realistically a Democracy by way of a Monarchy. Stated simply: It's a Democracy because the King allows it to be. The King of Thailand is the Monarch of the reigning Chakri Dynasty, in power since 1782, and the most recent reigning Dynasty in a long line of dynasties since the formation of the Monarchy in the 1200s. The late King "Bhumibol the Great" reigned for 70 years and is considered to be the most revered Thai King, and the longest reigning, in Thai history. After his passing in 2016, a 1-year mourning period was observed during which time the population wore black clothing and abstained from celebratory activities before his son, the current King Vajiralongkorn, took the throne. The Royal Thai family is said to be the wealthiest royal family outside of the Middle East, whose official home is the Grand Palace in Bangkok.

Thais hold the royal family in *very* high regard. You will see images of the King everywhere in public, and in every Thai home. The King's hymn will play before sporting events, concerts and movies, during which all in attendance must silently stand and show respect. You will see Thais pay homage to the King as they pass a statue or monument dedicated to the King. Respect for the King transcends daily life in the Kingdom.

As a tourist, you should be aware of this (it'll be very obvious) and be careful to never make negative remarks towards the King or royal family, as there are *Lese Majeste* laws in effect. Even in private, statements which could even be remotely interpreted as negative should be strictly avoided, as well as any lines of questioning (which I see often) targeted at Thais which have the potential to be mistaken for criticism of their devotion to the King.

An example of that would be asking a Thai something like "Do you think the King is a God?" or "Do you worship the King?" The answer is no, of course, but if these are the types of questions you have, keep them to yourself.

[17]

Similarly, Thais hold their religious figures in high regard as well. Images of Buddha are *officially* forbidden to be taken out of the country (to include statues and paintings, though you will see these for sale), Buddha tattoos are *officially* forbidden (but you can get one) and Monks are to be respected at all times and never touched physically (this one's real). When walking past a Monk, you'll see Thais duck their head down lower than him to show respect, and when walking past a Buddha statue, they will show respect with a *Wai* then as well.

You may notice some things that are forbidden aren't really forbidden. Reality always lies just below the surface here.

Cleanliness

Thais keep their bodies very clean (frequently showering multiple times per day) and are simply **disgusted** at body odor. And I do mean disgusted. It gets *incredibly* hot in Thailand, which means walking for just 5 minutes outside may get you sweating (and smelling) like you just played a game of football. With that said, you'd think they may be more forgiving to foreigners not used to the heat? Well…no. If you are stinking a bit and need to go to a meeting, dinner, or generally be in the presence of Thais, I would highly recommend being a bit late so you can shower, rather than go emitting an odor. Really. Body odor will instantly frame you in a negative light to Thais, which may or may not be too important to you as a tourist, but good to know either way.

If on the train in Bangkok (or any confined area) and someone enters with body odor, take note of the Thais reactions. It's truly comical. Even adults will sneer like schoolchildren.

Family

Thais put their family before anyone else in their life. Within the family, the elder members (usually parents, grandparents) come first, then children, then siblings. Thais commonly refer to their cousins and close friends as brother/ sister, which confuses many Westerners.

Thais have a stronger obligation than anywhere else I have seen on the planet to take care of their parents. It's a non-negotiable part of life. Thais wouldn't be able to fathom not taking care of their elder family members, almost as if that part of their brain is missing. If a choice had to be made (and certainly it happens) between feeding the kids or the parents, the parents would be fed and the kids would not. This would happen without a single thought.

Live for Today

It is common among Thais to think and act very shortsightedly. Long term planning and the ability to forecast future impacts on their well-being from the decisions of today is a foreign concept to most Thais. This is a common gripe you'll hear from many foreigners living in Thailand about their native spouses, and one you can hear quite frequently being discussed among that demographic.

- *Example A: A taxi driver wants to charge you 150 Baht (Thai currency) for a one-way trip. You explain to him that if he lowers the rate to 75 Baht, you will hire him every day that week for the same route. He refuses, not because the price is too low, but because he would rather have the instant gratification of 150 Baht that day than the additional income the following 4 days.*

- *Example B: You are negotiating with a Thai company to import a product into a new country. This expansion could mean doubling their revenue within one year. They are currently netting a 50% profit margin on their products at wholesale prices. You need them to come down on their wholesale prices in order to recoup importation costs plus gain entry into and compete with the local market. This would lower their profit margins to 40%, but they would double their market value. They choose to not drop their price.*

As you can see from these scenarios (all from my own experiences) it is very common in Thailand for people to be unwilling to give up something today with the prospect of a bigger return tomorrow. Whether or not this is due to the generational mindset from a low-income agrarian background many Thai families come from or rooted in the Buddhist teachings to "enjoy what you have today because it might be gone tomorrow" is out of scope for this book. Though this mindset does have some positive benefits when you think about it from the Buddhist standpoint, it will drive you nuts if you spend much time around Thais.

The Body

Thais have a few strange quirks and beliefs concerning the human body. Many of these are based in the particular form of Buddhism practiced in the country, Theravada Buddhism, as well as what many say are infusions of bits and pieces of beliefs and superstitions dating from the pre-Buddhism times. This is what makes Buddhism in Thailand unique to other places and why certain body parts are considered dirty, certain parts are holy and some gestures can be considered very rude. Generally, the higher up on the body, the more sanctified that part of the body is considered to be. (Think back to how a *Wai* placed higher up on the body is more respectful than a lower placed one.)

Thais do not like to be touched on the head. The top of the head is considered the most sacred part of the body. As hard as it is, you must refrain from ruffling those adorable kids' heads. Their Mother won't be very happy about it.

Thais also don't point at things with their fingers or use a finger to signal "come here" as you might in your country. Instead, they will either point with their entire hand or their chin. To signal "come here" they will use the whole hand, palms down, and wave their fingers in like they are scratching a dog's head or waive the entire hand downward at the wrist (This is the same throughout Asia). No one is very certain of the reasons for this, but it is disrespectful to use your fingers towards people (objects or animals is fine, which is why if a Thai points at you with their finger, please consider it an insult).

Not surprisingly then, the feet are considered the least-clean of the body. I probably don't have to tell you at this point to not use your feet to point at someone, but in addition to that it's considered general bad manners to use your feet for just about anything other than walking, such as moving something or even sitting with the bottom of your feet exposed to someone. Thais also *always* take their shoes or sandals off before entering a home. You won't see this as much in Bangkok, but if you get out to the rural areas (what I like to call the *real* Thailand), it will become very apparent to you.

If feet are so disrespectful, why is it that foot massage is such a widely perfected profession in Thailand? The world will never know.

Skin Tone

Thais have a peculiar fixation with skin tone, which is shared amongst most Southeast Asian races. In short, they are slightly obsessed with having light skin. This can be traced to the cultural divide between the non-working ruling class and the rice farming populace going back thousands of years. As a result, Thais see light skin as a symbol of status. It's ingrained in their psyche going back centuries.

So it is because of this fixation on skin tone, that Thais take great care to keep or obtain light skin complexion. They wear long sleeves and pants in 120-degree heat, avoid the sun like a vampire, and buy all manner of whitening cream and skin products promising to make them lighter.

Thai Women aren't the only ones. Thai Men also have this fixation. Don't be alarmed by the men in ski masks or camouflaged hoods during the day. It's a Thai motorcycle taxi driver or landscaper doing his job and trying to not become dark.

How Thais View Foreigners

"In Thailand, foreigners are to be treated well, but taken advantage of at

every opportunity."

-A Wise Man

Let me tell you here and now, no truer words have ever been spoken about the Land of Smiles. He was referring to the 2nd national sport (after Muay Thai) of parting unsuspecting tourists, and some expats, from their cash. The Thai tourism machine is designed to leverage the allure of their country to benefit the economy in any way possible, from the top all the way down to the beach vendors and foot massage ladies. Let them know you are aware of the game being played, and you'll fare better than most.

The intent here is not to instill a preconceived negative mindset about Thai people. Far from it, Thai people are absolutely wonderful. There is a stark difference, however, between your average Thai and those that work in the tourism economy. These peoples' livelihoods depend on keeping up the paradise façade and making sure the tourist cash machine stays well oiled. Keep in mind that foreigners only began to visit Thailand in large numbers in the 1960's, when the new tourism economy began to pick up steam and many Thais began associating foreigners with the influx of money they brought with them. This is *basically* still the case today, as some Thais have a habit of assuming foreigners *never* have any of their own financial issues, and money grows on trees where they come from. This assumption is common both in and outside of the tourism zones.

The first significant contact Siam had with a European colonial power was with the French. When the French colonized Cambodia and Vietnam, the Thais pronounced "France" as *Fa-ranc* due to their dialect not being able to put certain English letters directly together (for example, the name Scott is pronounced "Sa-cott" and so forth.) In the years since, **Farang** has become the de-facto term for foreigners in general, no matter the origin, color or creed.

Unfortunately, Thais (being a bit judgmental as we have discussed) tend to judge most Farangs based on a number of things, right off the bat. When you meet Thais, they will try and determine a few things about you in order to place you on their mental social ladder, which then enables them to proceed with their interactions (or non-interactions) with you accordingly. Keep in mind this is not me, this is years of experience in the country talking, so let's not get offended here:

Backpacker: Identified by your European, Australian or American origin, aged 20-40, dressed for hot weather at all times and probably staying at a hostel and can't wait for that Full Moon Party. Tourism centered Thais won't care to be overly friendly, because you are probably on a limited budget and can't spend money, but that won't stop them from trying. Normal Thais won't care too much about you either, simply because you'll be gone soon. They'll all be superficially friendly, but don't expect anyone to remember your name.

Digital Nomad: You are becoming quite common in Thailand, identifiable by your camera equipment and working from your laptop in public. You could be from anywhere, typically aged 20-30 and perhaps a bit of money coming in. Thais may be drawn to you for your youthful energy, or for no other reason than to gain popularity, as they have a fascination with all forms of social media. It's also assumed that you may be in the country for a longer period of time, opening up more doors for you with the local community.

Wealthy Businessman: Simply dressing nicely will earn you the respect of Thais based on first impressions. They will assume you to be here on business, and not "holiday," placing you as a potential friend, business connection or at least someone they want to know. They'll smile at you and talk about you when you leave.

Sex Tourist: A darker side of tourism in Thailand. You're identified not by your country of origin, but by your 40 and over age, casual attire and the scantily dressed younger woman you're walking around the Sukhumvit area of Bangkok with. You're more than willing to be relieved of your money and consistently are. Tourism centered Thais will shower you with love hoping to gain some of the money you're freely parting with. Normal Thais despise you, as they hate the perpetuation of this negative image of their country and want no association with you. Most Thais will smile at you but are stabbing you in the back with their minds.

Short Term Visitor: Aged 20-50, not a backpacker, businessman or sex tourist, but gainfully employed somewhere, and probably in the country for a few weeks to see the sites and enjoy themselves, perhaps with a group of friends or spouse. Identifiable by your average dress and probably staying at a hotel or Airbnb. Tourism centered and normal Thais alike enjoy getting friendly with you and may even remember your name.

Expats, retirees and English teachers have been spared (unlikely to be reading this), but similar stereotyping applies there as well.

Modern Tourism

Over-Tourism

As mentioned in earlier sections, once the people of Thailand realized they could leverage the allure of their country for wealth, an economy devoted solely to capturing the opportunities presented by tourism emerged. Over the decades, this machine has been finetuned to operate with precision, with each cog in the wheel doing its part to bring in more people and more money, while maintaining the image of the paradise most tourists envision it to be.

So focused have efforts been to grow the tourism trade, that basic infrastructure needs are almost always grossly overlooked, eventually bringing some fairly gruesome facts to the forefront of the façade created by the tourism machine.

For example:

- **Bangkok** is sinking at a rate that will have it below sea level by 2030, all due to the exponential addition of high-rise hotels and condos, yet developments proceed still.

- The former fishing village of **Pattaya**, once famed as an R&R spot for American GI's on holiday, has become such a high-density cesspool that the municipal infrastructure can't handle the ever-increasing water and waste loads placed on it.

- **Ko Phi Phi**, the famed beach from the movie "The Beach" has been shut down indefinitely (at time of writing) due to "over-tourism" (a term almost certainly coined in Thailand).

Such issues underscore the previously discussed lack of planning that unfortunately permeates the otherwise beautiful culture, and the tendency to take action and recognize an undesirable problem only when a crisis occurs. But, I bring this up to point out that expanding the tourism trade has always been a priority relative to other supplemental matters. It's a practice that's worked great until recent years.

Currently, plans are in the works to both expand the airport capacity for incoming arrivals to almost double what it is, as well as add a high-speed direct rail link to China, which will (as certain as the sun sets) increase the numbers of Chinese tourists (already increasing exponentially) to unfathomable levels.

The machine Thailand has created which keeps its tourism income high, and maintains the paradise façade, will soon begin to cannibalize itself as the number of tourists become unsustainable. Prices are already becoming high enough to warrant consideration of alternate destinations (Hello Philippines!) and the high-rise condos that are sinking Bangkok continue to go up at a breakneck pace, despite the fact that a great portion of the pre-sales funding construction come from foreign investors (Hi again China) who may never step foot in them.

With all that said, Thailand remains a magical place, and plenty of destinations in the country aren't nearly the horror story I described above. The country *IS* taking steps to mitigate these issues, as it has become beyond the capability of the tourism industry to hide. In later sections, I will give you some recommendations for some of the most beautiful places to visit, some that have not yet reached the crisis point, and some that likely won't ever get there.

Tourism Demographics

Having established the fact that Thailand is clearly a popular place to visit, here are a few rough statistics to ponder:

- The Thai Ministry of Tourism expects a record 40 Million visitors in 2019, which is more than half the population of the country.

- The majority of tourists visiting Thailand come from China, exceeding 25% for the past few years and increasing rapidly, with Malaysia, Russia, South Korea and Japan following.

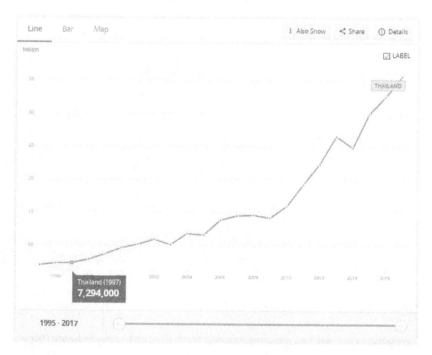

Tourism Seasons

As with most places in Asia, the tourism seasons roughly match the weather patterns.

Dry Season/ High Season lasts from around October to April, the weather is much better, and plenty of travelers tend to flock here during the Winter. Prices for everything are at their highest during this time and expect crowds wherever you go.

Rainy Season/ Low Season is usually the months between May and October, when you can be reasonably certain that it will rain every day at some point, usually in the evening. Monsoon season peaks in late Summer/ early Fall and can be prolonged in the south after things start to dry up in the north. Expect prices to be the lowest during this time, with some tourism operations closed around the beaches. The plus of traveling during this time is that there are MUCH fewer crowds and you can negotiate practically anything down. Just bring an umbrella out, even if there's not a cloud in sight when you head out for the day.

Popular Tourism Areas

With plenty to do, here is what most people come to do while in Thailand, and where they tend to do it at:

Beaches: The best and most popular beaches in Thailand can be found along the West coast on the Andaman Sea, with a few popular places inside the Gulf of Thailand. Some of these are discussed in detail later, but the most popular and heavily visited are:

- Southern Thailand: Phuket, Koh Samui, Koh Tao, Koh Phangan
- Krabi, Hua Hin, Pattaya, Rayong

You'll have plenty of company at these locations.

Temples: Bangkok is home to hundreds of temples, new and old, and are sure to be packed with tourists. The ancient capital of Ayutthaya, just north of Bangkok, has many older temples as well and should be on your list, as should Chiang Mai in the North.

National Parks: Plenty of beautiful scenery exists away from the ocean, complete with the tall cliffs you've seen photos of, caves and wildlife.

Wildlife: Thailand is home to a number of Elephant sanctuaries and zoos, many where you can interact very personally with the animals.

Healthcare: Thailand is a popular destination for healthcare as well, for the internationally trained doctors and highly affordable cost of medical services

Shopping: In addition to the many markets, tourists are visiting in high numbers specifically to shop at the many luxury malls being developed in Bangkok and other cities.

Whatever you may be visiting Thailand for, you're sure to be spending money, thereby contributing your share to the Thai economy, naturally. With that understanding, you should always be aware that, to the locals plying the tourism trade, you'll be looked at as simply a new source of income. In whatever sector of the economy you're playing in: Play the game and play it well.

The Golden Rules for Negotiating in Thailand

Staying within these negotiating parameters will ensure that you consistently don't get *too* screwed over on pricing when shopping at a market, negotiating transport or otherwise transacting with money. Not all settings are appropriate to begin a negotiation; however, so please don't enter reputable brick and mortar establishments and start haggling with waitstaff or hotel clerks (Yeah, I'm looking at you India).

1. ***Agree on a price BEFORE accepting goods or services:*** This may seem obvious, but it is imperative to agree on a price before going further. That means, don't get angry when a taxi driver asks an outrageous fare after the ride is complete, when you failed to agree on a price before-hand. Clever locals will take advantage of this if you give them the opportunity, but *very* rarely will a Thai go back on their word. Once an agreement is made, you should have a high level of confidence it will be honored. This also means not haggling over the price of a meal after you've eaten it (Still looking at you India).

2. ***Don't tip your hand:*** Don't openly count your wad of 1,000 baht notes when you're about to get into a negotiation over an item that costs 300, and don't show it after either. Use some common sense.

3. ***Never make the first offer:*** Get a baseline first, then proceed with below.

4. ***When a price is given, counter with 1/3 of that.***

5. ***The agreed upon price will end up around 2/3 of what the asking price is.***

Example: 300 baht is asked for an item. You say no, 100. They say 250, you say 150, they say 200, you have a deal, or something thereabouts. Thais know what they'll accept for things and will structure their first asking price exactly like this, asking a 50% markup.. Every. Single. Time.

Note: Just because you know the price will end up at 200, don't start with that or it will end up closer to 275. They follow this structure like they were trained from birth no matter what your counteroffer is.

6. ***Introduce competition:*** Take a look at the competition for an immediate price drop.

7. ***Walking away is a negotiation tactic:*** If 2/3 of the asking price is still too high, walk away. If there was any fluff in the other party's numbers, they'll come down. If they don't, that's really as low as they can go.

8. ***Don't show emotion or anger:*** As is typical, remain calm in your daily dealings. Nothing positive comes from losing your cool when in Asia.

These are the basics. Master them and you'll be able to get in and get out of any monetary transaction within seconds while other people are still trying to figure out where their wallet is.

Preparations

Toiletries

For the most part, you can find anything you need at the many 711 stores in Thailand, the department stores such as Robinson (most common) and the giant malls scattered around, so no need to use valuable space in your bags for common items. Some items you may have trouble finding, won't come in a type that you are familiar with or that you should stock extra of, are listed below:

- **Deodorant:** For some reason, not a huge variety of Western-style deodorant is available in Thailand. This has always baffled me, as it will baffle you now that we've discussed Thais' hatred of body odor. Bring your own.

- **Sunscreen:** Thais aren't big into allowing their skin to be touched by the sun, as we know, and the sunscreen market isn't the same as you might be used to, as Thais tend to wear long sleeves and hats to deal with the sun. While still somewhat available, the name brands you may be used to are priced up very high (Thais don't buy Banana Boat... foreigners do, so it's more expensive) and the local brands, meant mostly for the face, are either mixed with lotions, scented or otherwise

not attractive for a male to wear. Ladies, you might be ok with it.
Either way, pack your own.

- **Mosquito Repellent:** This is available at 711 in small pump-spray bottles, but make sure you bring the type with DEET. Mosquitoes will eat you alive in some parts of Thailand, and the diseases they can spread are not uncommon, or pleasant. Carry it out with you and apply even in the daytime, and even in the cities. Thai mosquitoes are the special forces of the insect world.

Though you can pick up most things in Thailand, I also recommend making sure you always have a few items on hand while traveling between places:

- **Baby Wipes:** The heat, walking, and sweat takes a toll. Keep these around for when you need it or bring it from home.

- **Toilet Paper:** Ok, don't carry a whole roll of TP with you, but pick up some of the smaller travel sizes at 711. Most public restrooms won't have free TP, if any.

- **Aloe Vera:** Better to have this when you need it. Nothing is worse than a bad sunburn, and in this part of the world, those are easy to get. Also overpriced in Thailand, and sometimes ineffective.

Healthcare

As mentioned briefly, healthcare is an area that you may actually be better off with in Thailand than at home. The country has become a destination not only for the beaches, food and weather, but **healthcare tourism** is a booming sector, with world-class facilities and internationally trained and credentialed doctors at incredibly cheap prices. Especially in Bangkok, major private hospitals are providing every type of service and procedure under the sun, in a very efficient, organized and systematic way to a *mostly* foreign patient base for a fraction of the cost than most of these peoples' home countries. Not in scope for this book, but if you or someone you know is considering a procedure, or has a condition which requires an operation, it may be worth looking into. The cost of the flight can be more than recouped by the savings from the operation in many cases. Plus, after recovery, you can go hit the beach.

Now, my point is, you will be ok medically if you experience an accident or require healthcare services during your trip. All decently sized hospitals, both in Bangkok and in the smaller cities, have English speaking doctors and staff available. I would still recommend making sure your insurance covers you during your trip though, just in case of a real emergency.

Medications and Pharmacies

As far as medications go, you should bring enough from your country to last you while you're here, and make sure you have the prescription with you in case questions arise. If there's a chance you'll run out, or if you want to pick up some much cheaper than your home, double check the legality of the particular medicine online. Due to the low cost, many people do stock up on medications while in Thailand. For this reason, we'll go over how best to do this in some detail.

It is worth noting that small pharmacies are a dime a dozen in most Thai towns and cities. To the untrained eye, it would also seem that many regulated drugs are available at these pharmacies without prescription, and for cheap. This is rarely what it seems. Many of these pharmacies sell knock-off medications (especially in the tourist zones), and even some of the medications being sold can be illegal in Thailand. Worse, you'll occasionally hear about the Police staking out a pharmacy and busting unsuspecting people (we'll get to the Police later) who may have not even known the drug they were buying was even illegal in Thailand. I have actually heard of people getting in trouble for buying fake drugs, which are supposed to be illegal, from a seemingly reputable pharmacy. (This is when someone with experience in the country would remark something like "Welcome to Thailand.")

A general rule of thumb with pharmacies is: If the pharmacy is inside a mall or department store, it's 100% guaranteed to be licensed. If not, you're probably safe buying over-the-counter (OTC) meds there, but nothing that should require a prescription (See *Tip* below). Also, the pharmacies around the major hospitals do usually have a better selection than others.

If you need prescription medication, you will need to visit a clinic or hospital and get a *real* prescription for it (Bringing along your prescription from home is a good idea.) If that's all you need, I recommend finding a clinic that will write one that you can pick up at any of the reputable pharmacies around such as Boots and Watsons. Ask in advance if they can do this.

Tip: *If you have gotten a prescription and are seeking a cheaper source than the hospital pharmacy or major chain, find a clean and reputable appearing pharmacy near a major hospital and ask for the subject medication. If they offer to sell it to you without a prescription, don't buy it here. If they tell you it is prescription only, you may then produce the prescription and probably get the medicine MUCH cheaper than you would have found it elsewhere. This is the only time I would recommend buying prescription meds at a non-hospital or chain pharmacy. You can also have the clinic call it in ahead.*

Below are a few OTC medicines that I recommend bringing along with you:

- **Benadryl:** I have never seen Benadryl in Thailand. Bring your own, especially if you are prone to allergic reactions (to anything).

- **Epinephrine:** If you're prone to allergies, better bring an Epi-pen along too. Many ingredients you've probably never had may go into your food in Thailand. Best to be prepared.

- **Ibuprofen/ Tylenol:** Bring your own.

- **Sleep Aid:** If you take anything other than natural supplements, bring your own.

- **Pepto Bismol/ Tums:** If you have a preferred type of antacid medicine, and aren't used to Thai food, I recommend you bring your own from home (and plenty of it) as these can be surprisingly hard to find, though you can find drinkable Maalox.

- On the same note, **diarrhea medicine** and probiotics may be a good addition to your medical kit as well.

Travelers' Sickness

It is common to get food poisoning, travelers' sickness, bacterial infection, "the crud" or other sicknesses while traveling in SE Asia requiring a regimen which includes (but may not be limited to) an antibiotic. Most antibiotics are available OTC in Thailand, BUT you should still see a clinic before self-prescribing. Not only are there too many fake meds out there, there are literally so many local types of infections that a local doctor will be able to make sure you're taking the right one, thereby lessening your recovery period and saving your good bacteria from being wiped out by numerous rounds of self-medicated trial and error antibiotics.

I also recommend drinking plenty of the small probiotic drinks available at any convenience store (Yakult is the most popular). These are claimed to be packed with probiotic and great to keep your good bacteria count up, which is needed to balance out the bad bacteria from your new environment, but also important if you're on an antibacterial dose to keep your intestinal tract bacteria in balance.

Tip: Another good way you can prepare for your trip, and possibly avoid getting travelers' sickness in the first place, is to begin taking probiotic supplements or eating yogurt each day in the weeks leading up to your trip.

Vaccinations and Diseases

You may now be thinking to reconsider your trip based on all of the information about getting sick and fake medications. Don't worry about it. Think if it as a badge of honor. No one goes to Southeast Asia and makes it out without a few health scares, besides, we haven't even gotten to the list of diseases.

Now, about vaccinations: You don't *NEED* to get them all, but it's always a good idea. In fact, if I was a doctor I would be obligated to recommend you *DO* get your vaccinations per my Hippocratic Oath to "prevent disease whenever I can."

Deciding on these will be highly dependent on where you travel to, and the types of activities you plan on doing. For example, if you plan to go straight to Koh Samui and spend your time between the beach and your room, you probably don't need to worry much about Dengue Fever. But if you're Elephant trekking through the jungle in Isaan (Northern Thailand) for 5 days... YES. Below vaccines are standard regimen prior to trips to the region:

- **Hepatitis A/ B:** Hepatitis A vaccines must be given twice over a 6-month period before they are effective; Hepatitis B vaccines are given once, with boosters every few years. Both are encouraged if you plan on spending time in SE Asia.

- **Typhoid:** Required every few years. You may or may not need based on your last vaccine date.

- **Japanese Encephalitis:** Required over the 30 days prior to your trip. Transmittable by mosquitoes.

Other diseases that are common enough to warrant your attention, but are either:

   a. low enough risk that you can address it post-exposure,

   b. prevent it by means *other* than a vaccination OR

   c. vaccination doesn't exist include:

- **Malaria:** Not all *too* common, and preventable by keeping the mosquitoes away. Malaria pills can be taken but must be taken for a time before and after your trip. Easier to use repellent if you ask me.

- **Dengue Fever/ Zika:** No vaccination exists. Again, keep those mosquitoes away. (See a pattern here?)

- **Rabies:** Vaccinations must start 30 days prior to your trip. If bitten by a dog seek medical attention ASAP. Street dogs are *VERY* common, but usually harmless unless interacted with. Leave them alone!

- **Sexually Transmitted Diseases:** Dogs aren't the only diseased creatures in the Land of Smiles, STDs are notoriously common in Thailand. Be safe, watch what you're doing and who you're doing it with. HIV is prevalent as are other life-altering diseases.

For more information on diseases and vaccinations in Thailand, visit the Center for Disease Control Thailand page for updates and specific guidance.

Emergency Numbers

These are going to be the same in any part of Thailand. I recommend programming these into your phone, along with pertinent numbers for your Embassy in the country.

Tourist Police   **1155**

Thailand Emergency Services (Fire, Ambulance)   191

The Tourist Police are specifically there for the purposes of liaising between the Thai Police and the large tourist community. They typically have a few retired/ expat Police from various countries on staff as well, so the language barrier will not be a problem.

Also, if you do get into a bad situation, mentioning the Tourist Police is *one* method to deter shady activity before it starts. I am *not* saying go around and threaten people with this, but if you're being really screwed over, at least you will appear to be a well-informed tourist.

Language

Due to the high numbers of visitors, English is a common language in the larger cities and coastal destinations in Thailand. Even the most poorly educated person will speak enough English to communicate effectively in their job if their job is anywhere near the tourism sector, and odds are if you come into contact with them, it is. English is not only the native language for the target audience of this book, but English is (and this may come as a surprise to some) how people from different *Asian* countries communicate also. That's right. Koreans, Japanese and Chinese people will also use English to communicate with Thais in most cases while on vacation or holiday (though many more Thais are learning Mandarin due to China's economic expansion and increasing tourism presence in the country).

I KNOW I am wrong for this, but it can be entertaining to catch a Thai and another Asian struggling to communicate in English when neither has a very good English ability.

Now, if you venture off the beaten path, to include the massive area of Isaan (Northern Thailand), this no longer applies. English is less commonly spoken here, and many people simply won't be very excited to try and communicate with you, as they are less likely to work in the tourism sector. This is when your means of communication will start to change from verbal to sign language, translation device or not at all.

Translation Apps

There is currently a multitude of mobile apps available to aid in translation, and I have found none of them to work well with Thai. I would recommend an app or device that has high reviews and is capable of working offline. When using any app, use simple sentences as the meaning can easily become very construed when translated into Thai. Keep it simple.

Do: *"Where is the train station?"*

Do not: *"Do you know where the nearest train station is."*

A few proven pocket translation devices do exist, which communicate effectively in both online and offline mode, which is crucial. As someone who has worked with numerous interpreters, the human aspect of translation is something most apps fail miserably at. For a list of apps and devices that DO work well, visit my resource page at **40MinuteTravelGuru.com**.

Critical Key Phrases

You should have a basic grasp of *some* Thai language to get by. For good in-flight reading, I recommend Survival Thai. Before we dig in, you must know:

1. Thai is a very *tonal* language. The content of what you say isn't as important as *how* you say it. After review of the minimum phrases below, peruse YouTube for some videos to help with your pronunciation.

2. The use of gender-dependent *courtesy* words are constant, required and follow each spoken phrase or sentence. These are **Krup** (Male) and **Ka** (Female). Almost everything that exits the mouth should be followed by one of these if you're intent is to not sound rude.

3. For a man, the pronunciation of **Krup** is tricky. Think of it as "K-lup" said very quickly.

4. When stated alone, both are considered an acknowledgment or even *Yes*.

Here are the phrases I would consider knowing at a ***MINIMUM***:

*   **Sawadee Krup/ Ka** *(Sa-wa-dee-k-lup/ kaa)*: Hello

*   **Kob Khun Krup/ Ka** *(Kob-koon-k-lup/ kaa)*: Thank you

*   **Sabai Dee Mai Krup/ Ka** *(Sa-bye-dee-my-k-lup/ ka)*: How are you?

*   **Chai Krup/ Ka** *(Chai-k-lup/ ka)*: Yes

*   **Mai o krup/ ka** *(My-o-k-lup/ ka)*: No thank you (This works well with street touts and hard tactics salespeople. Most tourists won't know this. You'll be left alone after saying this once, as opposed to saying NO five times.)

*   **Mai Ped:** Not too much spice (When ordering food)

*   **Kohr To Krup/ Ka** *(Khowoar-toed-k-lup/ ka)*: Pardon me/ sorry/ excuse me (Grab staff attention OR when bumping into someone)

*   **Mai Pen Rai Krup/ Ka** *(My-pen-lai-k-lup/ ka)*: No problem/ Your welcome/ No worries (As discussed earlier, a way to ease tensions as well as say you're welcome)

Driving in Thailand

As a foreigner, you'll need to have your International Driver Permit to rent or drive a car, but anyone with a license can rent a motorcycle or "Motorbike." However, before making the decision to drive either in Thailand, you'd be well advised of some facts that may make you reconsider, such as:

- Thailand is consistently ranked in the Top 5 most dangerous countries in the world to drive in, 2nd only to Libya in 2017 on the World Health Organization list of the worlds' most lethal roads;

- The driving rules (if any) and styles are completely different than what you're used to (you drive in the left lane but the wheel is on the right side); and

- As a foreigner, if you were to be involved in an accident, you open yourself up to a whole basket of legal and police trouble (think corruption) you'd rather not have, in addition to handling the irate Thai you've gotten into an accident with.

The majority of the road deaths in Thailand are from motorbike drivers. Though a widely popular way to get around, Thais and expats will all agree on the level of danger riding OR driving motorbikes poses. It's rare to find a Thai who's not been in at least one motorbike accident of some sort in their life, and they all know at least one person who's died that way. Spend enough time in Thailand, and you're sure to be witness to a horrifying accident at some point. So, while it may be easy to do, I would highly advise you enjoy your stay as a rider, not a driver.

Transportation

Every mode of transportation is readily available in Thailand, and incredibly low priced compared to the same transportation in almost every other place in the world. Any journey will utilize a combination of transport types, which I have broken down for you by the type you'll be most likely to use, and also made note of how the cost stacks up to other available modes of transport.

Taxis ($$)

Outside of Bangkok, taxis will be your go-to mode of transport for short to medium distances and (compared to Bangkok) are usually fairly straightforward. Taxis *in* Bangkok are not. Bangkok taxis can be quite maddening. They are almost *always* a negotiation. Traffic is horrendous, which makes negotiations even worse because it provides the drivers with a ready-made excuse to weave into their negotiation any way they see fit.

With that said, they *are* a necessary evil and the madness can be mitigated by following the below guidelines:

1. *Ask if the destination is ok prior to entering*. Thai taxi drivers are surprisingly selective and will choose their fares based on the best return on their time. Asking this will either serve as the start of negotiation (in which case you should move on if you can) or get you a head nod to enter, bringing us to the next step.

2. *Only use metered taxis and confirm prior to entering*. Taxi drivers in Thailand are *notoriously* famous for asking higher rates with tourists rather than using the meter. In recent years, the government has made an attempt to address this, and you *can* report them (technically) but many drivers still refuse to cooperate if they think they can get away with it. Let them know you're an informed tourist and you'll be ok. Make sure the meter is ON before allowing him to start driving.

3. *Offer a tip to get you there fast.* This may seem odd, but it will prevent the driver from taking you for a time-consuming ride, which he may want to do now that he can't ask for a high fee up front. Don't worry, a small tip will do, and you don't even need to agree to how much (the total will still be far less than if you'd allowed a negotiation to take place). It's the thought of a tip which will mentally trigger him to get you there quickly. I don't know about you, but I'll gladly pay an extra

20 baht for an hour of my time not spent in a taxi. (And 20 baht is more than enough for a tip).

4. ***Use your Apple/ Google Map or GPS.*** Now that you're in a metered taxi, you're not in the clear. Keep track of the route you're on (more on phone service later), both to make sure you're not being taken for a ride, and also that the driver is going where you need him to. Keep in mind that if he is lost, he will *never* admit it, but will continue to drive around in order to save face or ask another driver. You can easily help him out with your phone map if you need to, which does require you to have your location plotted. If he is *actually* lost, he will happily accept the help with a smile.

5. ***Negotiate when you need to.*** Sometimes, you'll need to give up hope of a metered taxi. In peak traffic times or during inclement weather, for example, Thai drivers (being acutely aware of the concept of supply and demand) will take the opportunity to ask higher fares, for which I am usually happy to pay the few cents more to get out of the rain or exhaust fumes, as I am sure you will be too.

Grab/ Uber ($$)

Grab and Uber have recently merged in SE Asia, which creates (in my mind) a great alternative to the hassle of negotiating with taxi drivers. Even better, this eliminates the risk that you'll get the "too much traffic" excuse since they confirmed the trip prior to pick up. You'll find that many taxi drivers also double as Grab and Uber drivers, making their cars discernable by the stickers in the windows. This allows you to easily skip the hassle of negotiating and gives you some recourse if they don't follow the rules or don't show up. They are also aware of this and generally behave accordingly.

Motorbike Taxis ($)

By far the most dangerous, thrilling and quick way to get around the dense Bangkok traffic for shorter distances. The locals utilize "Motorbike Taxis" to get to/ from the BTS (metro train) stations as a necessity, so you can find the motorbike taxi stands literally at the end of each street. Just look for the orange-vested guys hanging out on their motorcycles.

The motorcycle taxi drivers know the streets better than anyone around and speak enough English to take you where you need to go. Enjoy the ride but only recommended if you've got a bit of adrenaline junky in you and your health insurance is up to date. It will seem like chaos at first, but there is a strange method to the madness. A few common-sense tips that somehow still get screwed up by tourists are below:

- If offered a helmet, wear it.

- Hold on so you don't fall off.

- Keep your knees and your belongings tucked well inward to avoid car mirrors.

- Wear your backpack in the front.

- Don't stick your arm out to take a selfie. (Hello, Korea!)

- Agree on a price first.

- Don't anger the motorbike taxi drivers. They're a poor, volatile and tightly knit bunch.

Rail ($)

There are numerous rail systems in Thailand, both private and state-operated, and all are currently expanding at a very rapid pace. A high-speed rail system linking Thailand with China and Singapore is in the works, as mentioned before. The **BTS Skytrain** in Bangkok is expanding so quickly at the time of this writing, that they cannot replace signage fast enough to keep up with the additions of new stations coming online, just to give you a frame of reference. However, both the **BTS Skytrain** and the **MRT Subway** are *very* user-friendly, especially compared to other attempts at increasing user-friendliness in Thailand's transport systems.

BTS Skytrain (Bangkok): The BTS connects most major areas in Bangkok and runs above the main thoroughfares of the city. Very user-friendly with English signage and backlit maps above exits to show you where you are. Payment can be made at the kiosks, help desk or via the Rabbit payment card (recommended) available at the help desk in each station. I highly recommend the BTS in lieu of traffic any day of the week.

Tip: Even if you don't need to go anywhere, the BTS is always kept very cold. Great way to escape the heat for a bit.

MRT Subway (Bangkok): The MRT connects some of the areas not serviced by the BTS. Also user-friendly, the MRT intersects with most BTS lines but is operated by a different company. Payable by both Metro Smart Card, kiosk and help desk.

Airport Link (Bangkok): Skytrain line linking Suvarnabhumi International Airport and the city center (Phayathai Station) in about 30 minutes. This line has 5 stops in between and is operated by yet a 3rd company, which doesn't accept payments by either Rabbit or Metro Cards. For tourists, I recommend the single trip tokens available at the kiosks. Trains arrive and depart to or from the airport every 10 minutes from 0600-2400. If you're traveling heavy, I highly recommend a taxi or using a luggage service for your bags (discussed later). Also of note, taxi service is spotty at the Airport link stops, so while I recommend this going TO the airport, you may be stuck at the station waiting for a taxi when coming FROM the airport.

State Railway of Thailand: For travel to the rest of Thailand, the State Railway of Thailand operates 5 lines from Bangkok to locations across the country: North (Chiang Mai), South (Hat Yai towards Malaysia), Northeastern (Nong Kai towards Laos), Northeastern (Ubon Ratchathani) and East (towards Cambodia). All lines originate from Hua Lamphong Station in Bangkok, accessible via the MRT Subway line.

The railway can be a slow but very scenic way to get around. If you have the time, I do think it's quite the experience, not only for the scenery but for the local flavor. 3 different classes of train tickets can be arranged, Classes 1 through 3. I recommend an air-conditioned sleeper/ 1st class if taking a train over any significant distance, as it can get uncomfortable if you don't ($$). But for an experience, a 2nd or 3rd class ticket ($) will have you mingled in with the locals and give you some perspective into Thai life you may miss otherwise. I've had some good times doing just this and it can be a refreshing break to mingle and share food with regular Thais who've got no interest in taking advantage of you as a tourist for a change.. To book train tickets on the State Railway of Thailand system, a 3rd party ticketing agent is the best and easiest way. Visit my resource page at 40minutetravelguru.com for more.

Tuk Tuks ($$$)

If you've made plans to travel to Thailand, you're likely already familiar with (and perhaps excited to ride in) the infamous **Tuk Tuk**. For those that don't know, Tuk Tuks are noisy, colorful, exhaust fume emitting auto-rickshaws used as a means of quick transport around Bangkok and other urban centers in Thailand. Most first-time tourists can't wait to ride in one. Most expats and long-time visitors despise them AND the guys driving these little tourist traps.

Though they can be a bit of fun zipping through traffic, these are not governed by anyone except the "Tuk Tuk Mafia" themselves. And yes, it is by definition a mafia. Tuk Tuks coordinate their high fees, have agreements worked out with local shops to bring tourists there against their will, and push other means of transport out of the major tourist zones in order to monopolize those areas. For these reasons let me give you some pointers and insight:

1. ***Don't ride in a Tuk Tuk.*** Okay, I realize you may do this anyway, but after one ride, I guarantee you won't make a habit out of it. If you must though...

2. ***Never pay what you're asked to pay.*** Always follow the ***Golden Rules for Negotiating in Thailand***. The Tuk Tuk mafias have set rates in

each area, and it doesn't matter where you go within that area, the price will be the same. Most tourists will pay this fare. The real price is 2/3 of what was asked. As always, negotiate before you get in.

3. *Avoid the Tuk Tuks near the BTS station.* In general, this is where the most unsuspecting tourists will be looking for a ride. For this reason, you minimize your chances of being overly-scammed by walking a bit further down and looking for a passing Tuk Tuk (or God-willing a taxi or motorbike).

4. *Do not EVER agree to go to one of the shops the Tuk Tuk driver wants to take you to.* The Tuk Tuk mafia is paid commission on goods bought by tourists taken to these shops. The driver will tell you just to have a look, and that he gets free gas out of the deal. Don't fall for it. He may also offer a highly discounted daily rate for stops at the most popular sites, if only you pop into the tailor or jewelry shop to have a look. Just avoid this altogether and move on. Keep in mind, these shops won't actually pay them if you don't buy anything, so you're putting yourself in an awkward position if you actually enter one of these stores and don't intend on buying. Don't do that. There are other Tuk Tuks and transport methods around that won't do this if you search a bit.

*Tip: One scenario where it makes sense to take them up on this offer is if you plan on visiting a tailor or jewelry shop anyway. Bangkok does have many high-quality custom tailors with good prices. If you can consolidate your plans to get a free day of travel out of the deal, it may be worth doing.

Songthaew ($)

A pickup truck with a tall cover really, the Songthaew is a preferred and cheap method to get around in the rural cities and many beach destinations. These passenger vehicles make the same loop, over and over again, up and down the same streets. In some locations, an English map of the routes can be found on the side of the truck, other times not, in which case it would be wise to at least attempt to communicate with the driver to confirm your destination before entering. Either way, to enter, simply waive the truck down on the route, enter from the back, and ring the buzzer when you need the truck to stop. When it stops, exit, try not to get hit by traffic, then pay the 5, 10 or 20 Baht to the driver.

Water Taxis (Bangkok only) ($)

Boats really, but the Thais call them Water Taxis. The famous long boats speed up and down Bangkok's network of canals, ferrying sitting and standing passengers between stops located close to bridges and other transportation points. Now, this is a mode of transport that is NOT user-friendly for foreigners but is something you must try. It's a great alternative to traffic and traveling to and from locations not serviced by the BTS. These were literally a game changer for me when I found out how easy it was. Here's how it works.

To board: Line up and board. Once the boat departs, the attendant who walks along the outside of the boat will ask your destination. His English will not be good, so know in advance which point you'll be getting off at and tell him (clearly this will require some advance research on your part). Pay the fee (usually very low so if you get confused, hand him a 100 baht and you'll get change). Keep track of your path on your phone or ask the locals when to get off (the signs are not clearly marked). Avoid getting trapped in the middle, or you may end up taking a boat ride for longer than expected.

Bus ($)

Bus travel is by far the most common city-to-city mode of travel in Thailand, due to the low cost and frequent schedules for any and all direction of travel. Each small city and town has a bus station, and there are hundreds of independently owned bus lines operating between them (as is the case in most of Asia). A long trip may require multiple bus changes, which makes it very difficult to plan unless you book a ticket in advance, or book a direct sleeper or 1st class bus (usually only available for heavily trafficked locations).

The main bus stations in Bangkok are the Eastern Terminal at Ekkamai BTS Station and the Mo Chit Terminal near Chatuchak Market. Both will have the same routes, so it depends which is closer to you when choosing and booking, but the Eastern Terminal is right on the BTS line. You will need to remain alert to required bus changes and other stops along the way to make sure you get off where you need to. Keeping track on your phone map is recommended. Bus travel is pretty much the same as rail travel (State Railway) in both cost and time.

Ferry ($$)

As Thailand has many islands, odds are great that a ferry is in your future if your plan is to see them. If you're traveling to an island from Bangkok by bus or rail, you'll need to take a ferry at some point. Like buses, there are numerous ferry companies and schedules constantly change, so I recommend booking in advance.

Air ($$$)

Outside of bus and rail, domestic air travel is your final option for travel within Thailand. A few domestic airlines run routes between a few main cities and the 2 airports in Bangkok, as well as Phuket. A few include Air Asia, Nok Air, Thai Airways and Bangkok Airways to name a few. Luggage fees are a concern here, as most of these airlines try to be as low cost as possible.

Navigation

Now that you're familiar with the types of transport available, you'll need to learn how Thais organize their streets to effectively communicate your destination, as well as maintain a general sense of where you are. First, some terminology:

Soi: a *Soi* is a side street, branching off of the main road which has a typical (Thai) road name.

Example: Soi 31 would indicate side street #31. Soi 31 may intersect Bangkok Road, which would make it *Bangkok Road Soi 31* or *Bangkok Soi 31*.

That's pretty simple, but:

• A Soi can have its own Sois.

- Sois are even/ odd numbered, similar to addresses in some countries.

- If you see something like *Soi 15/1*, this means a new street was placed between Soi 15 and 16.

- Large Sois can also be named similar to a main road.

- A Soi may intersect with two main roads and will be referenced at each end based on which main road that end is closest to. What's unclear to most, is at what point in the street the name actually changes. In these cases, *Bangkok Soi 31* is also *Airport Road Soi 45*, or something to that effect.

What can I say? Welcome to Thailand.

The Internet

First and foremost, you'll need cellular service. I cannot stress this enough. You'll need to be connected to find your way around, plan on the go and (heaven forbid) for an emergency situation. Few things to note about cellular service, the internet, and connectivity in Thailand:

Internet Service is Terrible: You'll notice as you walk around, the communication cables in the country look comparable to spaghetti strung up just above head level, a nightmare for an electrical lineman trying to make sense of things and a code violation in most countries. This may or may not be why the internet is consistently going down, even in the nicest of hotels and accommodations. This is especially frustrating when you are required to log back onto hotel Wi-Fi each time the internet drops your connection.

Electricity "Brown-Outs" are Common: I would like to say that this is due to the ever-expanding population exceeding the power capacity, but I venture to say that there was never a time in Thailand that this was not a problem. The power goes out regularly, for a few minutes to a few hours, and yes, even in the nicest of hotels.

For these reasons, it's not wise to rely solely on cabled internet connectivity in Thailand. Though cellular service is sometimes susceptible to the same "Brown-outs" it is more dependable than Wi-Fi in most cases. For cellular service, there are a few options:

- Pick up a **SIM Card** at any cellular service stand at the airport, found immediately outside the arrival gates. This is very straightforward in Thailand as long as your phone is not locked (when your carrier has placed a lock on it thereby ensuring it cannot be used with another carriers' SIM card.) Check with your carrier prior to leaving to make sure this won't be an issue. Of the carriers in Thailand, most have tourist plans (they're good at catering to the needs of the tourist, remember?) for anywhere from a few days all the way to a month.

Rates are incredibly cheap (I mean the 1-month unlimited data for about 10 USD kind of cheap) and there's no reason to not have unlimited data while you're in the country. Calling plans are available as well.

- If for some reason the SIM option is a no-go, you can rent a **pocket Wi-Fi** from the same cellular carriers offering SIM cards.

- Bring a means to charge your phone on the go. Exploring in Thailand requires heavy phone application use which will quickly drain your battery. Do not be caught in transit without a means to find your way if you need to.

You should be able to connect to the free Airport Wi-Fi immediately upon exiting your plane. Connect to Wi-Fi when you can to save your battery, but don't rely on getting free Wi-Fi everywhere you go.

Accommodations

Thailand doesn't have a plethora of different types of accommodation as say, Japan does, so there's really not a whole lot of new things to explore. With that said, there are some tips you will need to know to get you along:

Hotels

The majority of tourists tend to stay in hotels, of which there are literally THOUSANDS to choose from in Bangkok alone. The standard rules apply, with a few local tips:

- The food, including breakfast, is usually pretty overpriced in most hotels. Look for this when you book, it may be cheaper to include it, it may not be.

- Like the food, if you have the hotel arrange transportation ahead of time, it will be a private service and also very overpriced.

- Take a business card from the hotel with the address. Keep it in a safe place. Never know when you'll need it.

- Use the safe.

- Many hotels will hit you with a deposit that you didn't know about. Keep the receipt (in the safe maybe?) you may need it when you check out if the hotel wants to be greedy.

For recommendations on hotels in the most visitor friendly areas of Bangkok visit 40MinuteTravelGuru.com.

Hostels

Thailand is a major backpacker destination, and there are TONS of hostels that cater to both that demographic as well as budget Asian travelers.

You'll find these mostly in the heavily trafficked tourist areas, with an especially large selection around Khaosan Road in Bangkok, Koh Samui, Koh Phangan, and Phuket.

Airbnb

Airbnb is *officially* illegal in Thailand, at time of this writing; however, like all *officially* forbidden things in Thailand, the business is *unofficially* thriving. There are a few reasons why Airbnb is illegal, the main reason being that the large hotel chains have been able to sway the elected officials, who in reality will turn a blind eye and not enforce the regulation for fear of upsetting all of the new condo investors.

Anyhow, due to the unprecedented amount of high-rise condo development in Bangkok, and other cities, you can find great deals on Airbnb that, in my opinion, are a much better value than many premium hotels. For example, it's common to find a 40 USD/ night condo that appears in all manner of ways like a 200 USD/ night hotel room (without the service of course). Keep in mind though, that you may not want to advertise the fact that you're an Airbnb guest, as many buildings do have policies banning Airbnb *(officially, of course)*. If you go this route, don't worry, you'll be educated on the matter by the host. A few tips:

- Read the reviews closely and make sure you're getting a unique unit. Many wealthy Chinese investors have bought up large portions of these condos and are, in effect, running large short-term rental operations under the authorities' noses. These are highly illegal and you could be severely disappointed when your unit isn't what it was in the ad, with little recourse to correct it.

- Airbnb rates ARE negotiable in Thailand, but you have to ask and it has to be for at least a week. If traveling in low season you can find amazing deals on Airbnb.

Money

The Thai currency is the Baht *(bot)*. At the time of writing, the exchange rate has fluctuated between 30-31 Baht/ 1 USD for nearly a decade. Just think 1,000 Baht = roughly 30 USD. Getting your money out while in Thailand should be no problem, but you'll want to heed a few money tips:

- Take note of the exchange rate if changing money. The best exchanger is usually Superrich Thailand with numerous kiosks around the train stations and malls in Bangkok. If you're only changing a few hundred dollars though, it really doesn't matter, just avoid the ones at the airport.

- Any and all ATM's will accept your foreign ATM, Debit or Credit card. Don't worry about that. This is Thailand, they make taking your money easy.

- Use good judgment when deciding to use your Credit or Debit card. Might want to pay cash if it's the least bit suspect (not that it is always going to be an option).

- Keep your cash well organized inside your wallet/ purse/ pocket. Cash notes come in 20, 50, 100, 500 and 1,000 Baht. You'll want to keep the larger notes separated from the smaller for two reasons:

  a) Quick access to smaller notes to pay for common things such as taxis, drinks, etc. You don't want to take up time sorting through your bills in traffic; and (mainly)

  b) Don't attract attention by pulling out a wad of 1,000 Baht notes when trying to find a 20. Good luck negotiating a price down or getting rid of that pesky bird saleslady! It's like showing your hand at poker. Bad tourist.

Movies and Television

There is surely no lack of movie or TV content on Thailand, either shot in and taking place there, or depicting life or travel there in some way. Some of my recommended viewing for getting a *real* insight into life there (and

for entertainment value) is below:

- Movies: Bangkok Dangerous, The Hangover II, The Beach, Ong Bak: The Thai Warrior, Only God Forgives

- TV: Amazing Thailand, Anthony Bourdain: Parts Unknown S3E7, Anthony Bourdain: No Reservations S5E13, Journey into Buddhism

Welcome to Thailand

Arriving in Thailand

The great majority of incoming travelers arrive at **Suvarnabhumi International Airport** *(Sa-varn-a-boom)* about a 45-minute drive (in no traffic) East of Bangkok. Some may come in via **Don Mueang Airport**, to the North or possibly even a direct flight to Phuket if heading there. My advice for getting to and from each international point of arrival is below:

Suvarnabhumi to Bangkok: Firstly, it would be smart to have your arrival card filled out prior to landing, as the immigration line gets very backed up these days. Once inside, getting through immigration and customs is basically a non-event as long as you don't state in your immigration form your intent to stay beyond your allowed time (30 days for most countries at the time of writing). At this point, and after getting set up with a new SIM card or Wi-Fi device (see Technology section) you have two options for getting into Bangkok from Suvarnabhumi: The Airport Link or taxi. Private car or transport is available through most hotels but as mentioned, is usually very overpriced.

1. **Airport Link:** Found on the lower floor of the arrivals hall, I recommend using the Airport Link elevated rail system only if you are

traveling light and can easily travel on foot with your luggage. The reasons for this being that each of the stations along the Airport Link are typically not well serviced by taxis (needed to complete the trip) and usually some walking is required to get to the adjoining BTS/ MRT stations for further travel to your accommodations. Also, the Airport Link stops running from 2400-0600. If you're traveling very heavy or between those hours, best to take a taxi *OR* use a luggage service for your bags.

2. **Meter Taxi:** Make your way to the street level of the arrivals hall and look for the signs posted for Meter Taxis, the typically short queue is situated in the middle. Ignore anyone asking you if you need a taxi on your way there. The Airport Authority has integrated a great system in recent years that eliminates the risk of being haggled by taxi drivers, utilizing a ticketing system. When you find the queue, take a ticket from the machine and proceed to the numbered lane as indicated on the ticket. Make sure the driver understands your destination, showing him on a map if need be, or providing an address or phone number to call. Have this prepared when you get there to save time. Otherwise, follow my guidance from the Transportation section in this book.

Don Mueang to Bangkok: As with Suvarnabhumi, traversing immigration and customs should be a breeze. Once through, and getting set up with cell or Wi-Fi service, proceed to the taxi queue. This is very straightforward at Don Mueang and the same concept outlined for Suvarnabhumi.

Phuket International Airport: Meter Taxi is probably your only option here, so observe the normal guidance on arriving, then find the Meter Taxi (clearly labeled) counter outside of arrivals.

Lockers and Luggage Services

Though not as convenient as a few other Asian countries, there are a few resources for storage and delivery of luggage, to or from either airport and at some of the larger malls and BTS stations (Bangkok).

- Lockers sized from small to large enough to fit a suitcase into can be found at nearly every BTS station; however, there is light capacity so don't make plans that hinge on being able to store your luggage there. The locker company is Lockbox, and you must first download their app to use their service. Look for the yellow lockers. Rates are reasonable.

- For storage at major malls, airports, and delivery between airports and your hotel, I recommend Airportel Asia. They have low rates and I have never had a bad experience, plus there is no app to download. This is a great way to be able to use the Airport Link in Bangkok and skip traffic if you have lots of luggage.

- If using these companies, be prepared to have your passport and make sure your luggage is lockable, if using delivery. Also, keep the receipt.

Unfortunately, luggage delivery and storage options vary by location, so check with these companies first about their service in other parts of the country, though you may not need it anywhere outside Bangkok.

Thai Police

The Boys in Brown, as referred to lovingly by the expat community for their dark brown uniforms. Be wary of any type of involvement with Thai police. As is common in SE Asia, the Police are frequently also the jury and judge, and VERY frequently also the fine clerk. What does that mean? It means that they don't have the same, how shall we say, *issues* that Western police may have with receiving money. This is not only with tourists and expats, but this is also how they are structured.

To put some fair perspective on it, Police in Thailand are easily motivated to go above and beyond the call of duty with additional funding required to carry out certain operations. For example, if a jewelry store owner has a problem with theft, they can easily have the police perform extra surveillance by shelling out a few bucks (or "protection money"). The Police Generals have fundraising campaigns to fund their way into office, and of course, those who bet on the winner fare better once the new Sheriff in Town sets up shop. Sounds crazy I know, it's just the way things are done here. You could think of them as the Mafia, and many people will say that the real Thai mafia *is* the Police. This is pretty accurate.

So, you can see how the relationship between Police and money isn't the same in Thailand, and while this way of doing things does have its' benefits, many Police do take advantage of this. Police will commonly execute mass ticketing operations of motorcycle riders for breaking helmet laws, all of whom hand over a few hundred baht which probably never sees a city coffer. You very well may get caught up in some extortion scheme or get shaken down for jaywalking (laughable in Thailand), and asked to hand over 200 baht or another small figure. My advice for these situations is 100%, without question: **PAY THEM! PAY THEM! PAY THEM! AND SMILE** □

Everyone knows a story of some guy, from some Western country, who got involved in some minor situation where he was asked to pay a few hundred baht, and refused, then arrogantly proceeds to demand his rights, and so forth. Well, this, of course, gets him into a Thai jail, this time with EVEN MORE people he is required to pay (each level the situation escalates to, more people to pay) until the situation rapidly spins out of control and it becomes a matter of saving face on the part of the Police. At that point, they are certainly not backing down OR admitting any wrongdoing. You will frequently see the end results of this on the news in Thailand, where the subject foreigner is put on television to publicly admit to a crime so ridiculously small it's ludicrous to be airing on TV, and all I can think is "Why didn't you just pay them?"

It's for these reasons that you should generally avoid situations that could be construed as illegal or those where you could be caught up in a sting, framed or set up (a common one is where Thais offer drugs to tourists, then the Police bust them and ask for money, which is then shared amongst the group). I tell many first-time travelers to keep cash stored on your person, that you won't spend, just for an emergency. Again, no court, no lawyers. Just pay them.

Besides bartering for petty fines with tourists, it should also be noted that the Thai Police generally like to avoid trouble or be put in a situation where they may need to solve something unpleasant. They love large drug busts and raiding illegal operations of other flashy types of crimes that they can physically stand over top of and point at on TV, but they're known for more than their share of "open and shut" type casework as well. For example, I would wager that Thailand is home to the most self-inflicted stabs to the back, and subsequent leaps off of balconies than anywhere else in the world. This is, of course, to say that they don't like to advertise a high murder rate and scare tourists, and don't particularly care to run around looking for suspects either, especially when they could be making highly lucrative traffic stops.

Laws

It may seem at first as if Thailand has no laws at all, and one would be forgiven for thinking such after a few days in country; however, there is an order to the madness that must be abided by to avoid harsh repercussions or, at the very least, those pesky "fines" we discussed. To make sure you don't get yourself into a legal situation as described above, you ought to know some of the basic laws:

Drugs: Though many prescription drugs appear to be sold here without a prescription, we discussed how that isn't always the case, to begin with, and you *should* have your prescription handy if you come into the country with them. Illicit drugs such as cocaine, heroin, methamphetamines, etc. have heavy jail time associated with them for personal use, and the death penalty on the table for being convicted of intent to sell. Marijuana (though some would naively think legal in Thailand) is certainly not legal, and also carries stiff penalties for personal use, worse for intent to sell. At time of this writing, there is talk about the legalization of marijuana on some level; however, that's far out of scope for this book.

Buddha: As mentioned previously, it is illegal to remove an image of Buddha from Thailand, desecrate a Buddha image in any way, or generally disrespect Buddha. Also, it is illegal to have a Buddha tattoo in Thailand (but you won't have a hard time finding a place, if that's your thing, make sense?)

Littering: It may be shocking after a walk around Bangkok (which isn't the cleanest, but *far* from the dirtiest Asian metropolis) that littering even the smallest piece of trash can get you fined by those Thai Police I spoke of. Letting cooking oil run down the drains and leaving chicken parts on the street is perfectly fine though, if you're a food vendor.

Helmets: Helmet laws ARE, in fact, in effect. It's just that Thais don't like to wear them much. Besides being a good idea due to the insane death rate from accidents, you can be stopped and fined for this, even if riding on a motorbike taxi.

Disrespect of the King: As mentioned before, this is a law, and they do take this seriously.

Prostitution and Pornography: You wouldn't think it if you're familiar with the bad image Thailand gets, but both actually *ARE* illegal and can be enforced.

Alcohol Restrictions: Alcohol consumption is restricted in public parks, educations centers, and sale is prohibited during late hours (though this applies only to most convenient stores and not bars and restaurants).

Dining and Drinking

Thais love to eat. You'd be amazed at the amount of food they can consume, actually, and maintain their image of slightly underfed but happy. Eating in Thailand is a cherished part of life, and eating with a group is a slow, personal experience. Rice is eaten with every meal (a common theme in Asia) and a meal shared amongst family and friends will consist of many dishes for group sampling. Chicken, pork, and fish are a part of every meal as well, with fish usually being served with the entire grilled fish, and chicken and pork being sliced and cooked with a vegetable dish. All of the dishes are sampled in fairly small portions, and continually mixed with rice, a perfect bite usually consisting of rice and one or more different dishes.

Thais eat with a fork and spoon, using the fork as more of a tool to scoop the food onto the spoon than to "fork" anything. Thais will eat out more so than at home, due to the low cost and ease, but if you get the chance to eat a meal prepared at someone's home, don't pass it up. Eating at street stalls is also very common, as will be apparent, and sampling many different dishes from vendors and eating at a street-side stall is a great experience. This how most Thais eat small meals almost constantly throughout the day.

Drinking is also a large part of the dining experience. Thais will order large bottles of local beer with an evening meal (or sometimes during the day), served with a bucket of ice. Yes, the ice is for the beer. It may sound strange, but iced beer will grow on you while in Thailand if you allow it to. Whiskey is also a drink of choice, served with Coke and ice as well. When dining out, there is typically a cart positioned next to each table, containing the beer, whiskey, and ice, for the staff to fill your drinks whenever it is empty.

Tipping

Tipping is expected in Thailand, even just a little bit. In fact, not tipping anything at all will cause some face-loss on the part of the Thai. Best to tip at least a bit. If paying a few hundred Baht for a meal, tip the loose change received or a 20 Baht note. If tipping a taxi driver for a 100 Baht ride, 5 or 10 Baht will do. Just the concept of being tipped *something* is what's important here to maintain balance.

The exception: If the subject Thai screwed you over somehow (Hello Tuk Tuk driver), and both you and they know it, this is the scenario where tipping nothing at all will be just fine. They'll be happy enough as it is having screwed you.

Nightlife

Already established as "The World's Playground," decades of experience entertaining thrill-seeking tourists mixed with the loose and fun-loving ways of the Thais has proven to be a successful recipe for truly epic nightlife, just as deserving on the list of "World's Best" as the temples, beaches, and spicy food. There are endless ways to let loose and have a great time after dark, with nightlife establishments and areas catering to every unique desire from every part of the world you could imagine.

While Bangkok is the epitome of this with the countless nightclubs, rooftop bars, and entertainment zones, the general theme is present all over the country, with each tourist destination having its own nightlife areas catering to the demographics most present in those locations, most covered later in the book. I would encourage a first-timer to explore all the nightlife that Thailand has to offer, as the Thais love to have fun, and you'll be welcomed practically anywhere you want to explore.

Besides the widely-covered tourism-centric nightlife, Thais themselves are renowned for their ability to let loose and party, a likely byproduct of the "live for today" mentality present mentioned earlier. I would highly recommend making some local friends and having them take you around to explore the nightlife less-frequented by the foreign crowds. Thais are big into large nightclubs and outdoor beer gardens, nibbling on snacks while the beer and whiskey flows, jamming out to live (and very loud) bands performing the uniquely upbeat and fun Thai music, that you can't help but be fixated by as a foreign visitor. I guarantee you'll be hooked on it.

Must Do Activities:

Some things you just have to do in order to get a well-rounded experience, even if it means fighting the crowds in order to do so. Nonetheless, you must do these in Thailand.

- **Eat Thai Food:** This is obvious, I know. But try to eat Thai food where Thais eat. Avoid the expensive Thai restaurants appealing to the tourist crowds. And one other thing, don't go crazy and eat Thai for every meal. You'll have traveler's sickness by day 2.

- **Play with Elephants:** But avoid the places who've been in trouble for Elephant abuse. Reputable Elephant tourism operators can be found with a bit of searching. Take an elephant ride around Ayutthaya if you head there.

- **Play with Tigers:** At the Siracha Tiger Zoo an hour south of Bangkok or the Tiger farms in Phuket or Chiang Mai. Fancy milk feeding a baby Tiger?

- **Sunset at Wat Arun:** In Bangkok. Best viewed from any of the hotel rooftop bars from across the river.

- **See the Temples:** Obviously. The temples in Bangkok and Chiang Mai are the best. Dress appropriately (no shorts or sandals) when visiting the Grand Palace in Bangkok.

- **Ride a Tuk Tuk:** I know I said never to do this but…just don't visit the stores.

- **Tour Ayutthaya:** Via a day trip from Bangkok.

- **Ride a Water Taxi:** Around the canals in Bangkok.

- **Ride a Motorcycle Taxi:** Wear a helmet and hold on. Tuck those knees in and pray.

- **Get a *Real* Thai Massage:** Look for somewhere that does not have massage ladies trying to force you in. They aren't *Real Thai Massage* professionals.

- **Have a Traditional Dinner with a Thai Family:** If you know one.

- **Watch Muay Thai:** At **Rajadamnern** or **Lumphini** stadiums in Bangkok. Don't get the VIP seats. Get the 2nd class, the view is better and the cost is less.

- **Try Muay Thai:** Muay Thai gyms are scattered all over Bangkok and Phuket nowadays, and many offer lessons to beginners.

- **See a Cultural Show:** Siam Niramit is worth a few evening hours in Bangkok.

- **See a Ping Pong Show**: If you're up for it. Any Tuk Tuk driver will be more than happy to take you and collect their commission. Or, just walk around Patpong after dark and you'll be offered one.

- **Bangkok Rooftop Bars:** Bangkok is the King of rooftop bars. Catch the famous sunset while sipping a cocktail as the lights of Bangkok start to change the mood of the entire city.

- **Eat Street Food:** Just make sure to minimize your chances of bacterial infection by avoiding spotty looking vendor stalls. Chinatown in Bangkok is where the best street food can be found.

- **Floating Market:** A bit overrated if you ask me, and very crowded, but you could do a day trip there from Bangkok. Not for me, but I seem to be the minority, so you should probably see it.

- **Night Markets:** More than simply a market, where Thais and tourists go to unwind, eat and drink. There are many throughout the country, and a great way to mingle with the natives.

- **King Cobra Charmer:** Most common in Isaan, but a few exist in the tourist areas.

- **Take a Peek at the Seedy Nightlife:** Go take a peek in a Go-Go Bar in Soi Cowboy, Patpong Night Market, Soi Nana, Patong or Pattaya. Guaranteed to shock and amuse.

- **Celebrate the Thai New Year** (Songkran Festival): Celebrated at different dates throughout April. Popular for tourists in Bangkok, Chiang Mai, Phuket, and Pattaya. The wildest celebrations occur on

Khaosan Road in Bangkok, Nimman Road in Chiang Mai and Beach Road in Pattaya. But this is also when the road fatalities and general drunken shenanigans are highest, so be careful.

- **Celebrate the Loi Krathong Festival** (Rising Lanterns): Most notable in Chiang Mai, but celebrated throughout the Kingdom in early November.

- **Visit the National Parks:** Khao Yai National Park, Kaeng Krachan National Park, and Doi Inthanon National Park, to mention a few.

- **Diving and Snorkeling:** If you're heading south to Phuket, Krabi, Koh Samui or other islands, you've got to go diving. Some of the best diving in the world is found in these beautiful waters. If you're inexperienced, almost any place worth diving has multitudes of PADI certified dive shops to get certified for a fraction of what it costs you back home.

The Rules

Now, the culmination of all of the cultural sensitivities and unique limits to appropriate behavior one should be aware of. These things have been learned over the course of my extensive time in Thailand, through many relationships with Thais, both as family members and friends. If you heed this advice and stay within these parameters of behavior, I guarantee your time in the Land of Smiles will leave you with a smile.

- Observe and mimic the locals. If they aren't doing it, you probably shouldn't do it either. This is ok though because it's Thailand, and the locals do a lot of fun stuff.

- Take off your shoes when entering a home.

- Respond to a Wai, with a Wai.

- Respond to a smile, with a smile.

- Refrain from touching or hugging people that you have not gotten to know. Handshakes are not common, but acceptable. A Wai is better.

- Refrain from touching anyone on the head.

- Refrain from pointing at or waving at anyone with your finger.

- Use your wrist to signal "come here" and point with your entire hand or a slight head upward chin nod.

- Be patient and remain calm in your everyday dealings.

- Always smile when speaking with Thais.

- If a Thai offers to pay a bill, let them pay. If they offer you to drink with them, accept. Don't offer to split the bill, as this insinuates that they can't afford to pay it. Let them bask in their glory.

- If you invite someone, you pick up the bill.

- Keep your money segregated by bill value.

- Don't count your money in public.

- Don't cause a Thai to lose face. Ever.

- Don't get into a fight with a Thai. They will win.

- Don't make the first offer.

- Don't drink the water. Make sure your water is bottled.

- Don't pet the wild dogs. They bite and they likely have rabies.

- Be wary of unlicensed pharmacies.

- Wear mosquito repellent and take it out with you to reapply.

- Don't eat raw vegetables that could have been washed in tap water. Avoid salads at even nicer looking restaurants unless they tell you its safe. Cooked vegetables are fine.

- Avoid street food.

- Drink responsibly and watch your drink. Take it to the bathroom with you if alone. Drugging is not common, but it's not uncommon either. To be clear: Remain in control of yourself.

- Carry an Epi-pen if you have allergies. There's a lot of ingredients in Thailand.

- Don't drop money and not pick it up. The money has the image of the King, and Thais are offended when you do this. Pick up even the smallest coin.

- Avoid talking about the royal family unless you have something positive to say.

- Agree on a price BEFORE accepting goods or service.

- Make Thai friends to go out with.

- Pour others' drinks when they pour yours.

- Use the BTS and MRT when possible (Bangkok)

- Book your accommodation in Bangkok near a BTS or MRT stop.

- Outside of Bangkok, stay near the City Center, or near a large mall to ensure access to taxis.

- Avoid Tuk Tuks, and ride motorcycles at your own peril.

- Don't ever agree to be taken to a shop by a Tuk Tuk driver.

- Refer to elder Thai people you meet by *Kuhn* "Their name" if you want to appear respectful.

- Take only the metered taxi. Look for the **GREEN** light in the taxis, not the **RED**.

- Don't put yourself in a situation that opens you up to harassment by the police. This includes breaking any of the laws discussed.

- Tip everyone at least something who provides a service to you.

- Don't ever put yourself in a situation where you can't pay. Take extra cash with you everywhere.

- If the police fine you for something, pay them. Pay them. Pay them.

Bangkok

The Big Mango. The Venice of the East. The Gateway to Asia. In Thai, *Krung Thep* or "City of Angels." Bangkok is many things. It's dense, noisy, polluted, chaotic and beautiful. It's ancient and modern at the same time. The culmination of generations of rice farmers and traders colliding with the modern age. Walking just 1 block in Bangkok and you will experience 15 different smells, each more pungently offensive or curiously amazing than the next. You'll walk past skyscrapers going up faster than they ever should, towering over tin metal roofed markets that have been there for decades, and see people from every country on the earth living, working and experiencing what I consider easily the most interesting city on the planet.

Getting Around

Though we briefly covered this previously, let's get a bit more in depth. The preferred methods for travel in Bangkok are, in order of most to least desirable: BTS/ MRT, Taxi, Motorbike, Water Taxi, Walk. Tuk Tuks are excluded for reasons already discussed, and buses are omitted because I assume that if you're traveling, you can afford a taxi. (City buses are very cheap but hot and slow).

- **BTS/ MRT:** The BTS and MRT should be taken any significant distance, and anytime there is heavy traffic (which is most of the time but heavier during typical rush hours). With that said, the lines do not service all areas, and you'll be lucky if stops are located directly at your hotel, so you'll also need to utilize other means.

- **Taxi:** Taxis can be waived near any and all BTS stations. I suggest following the previously discussed guidelines for taxi travel.

- **Motorcycle Taxi:** The preferred means of all Thais to get from the BTS stop to their residence.

- **Walking:** You will do plenty of walking. This may seem odd, but I feel obligated to share a few *Bangkok Walking Tips* here (also applicable elsewhere in Thailand):

1. *Avoid sandals.* If walking very far. Yes, it's hot and you're in vacation mode, but the many street puddles you'll see are full of some atrocious stuff, and the sidewalks are full of hazards.

2. *Watch where you walk.* Bangkok sidewalks are notoriously uneven, with drainage caps frequently left loose, sidewalk repair occurring with no safety barriers and street mosquitoes concentrating their efforts in the 6" space above the pavement.

3. *Look both ways.* When crossing, even with a green light, watch out for turning cars and motorbikes, they won't stop just because their light is red.

4. *Just walk on out.* When crossing a street, you need to be able to walk on out into the traffic sometimes, as it may never fully stop. When you do, maintain course, and the traffic will adjust. DO NOT stop and panic and change course, this will get you hit and probably in a fight with the driver. Go with the flow. Watch how the locals do it.

5. *Ignore street touts.* When walking in any major tourist area, you will get lots of unwanted attention. Ignore and keep walking. They'll leave you alone. This includes unsolicited photos: If someone offers to take your photo, do not let them unless you are willing to pay (Mostly around the temples).

Neighborhoods

Bangkok is a massive city, to say the least. Within it, there are enough sub-cities and neighborhoods to devote an entire book on. As a foreigner, you won't need to explore every corner of Bangkok, but as an educated visitor, you'll need to know about the main areas at a minimum. Below I will provide some information on each of the major areas you need to know about.

Sukhumvit

The **Sukhumvit** (*Soo-khum-wit*) area of Bangkok is a happening place. Sukhumvit Road runs into downtown East to West and is considered one of the primary thoroughfares in the city. Along Sukhumvit are many smaller neighborhoods, each with their own character and reputation. Outside of the backpacker community on Khao San Road and sightseeing the temples in Old Bangkok, most of the foreign expats and tourists can be found around Sukhumvit. For this reason, and due to the accessibility and sheer volume of things to keep you occupied, you can't go wrong deciding to stay around here. Notable areas (branded by the relevant BTS stop) include:

- **Thonglor:** Heavy Japanese influence, many upscale nightclubs, trendy restaurants and bars. Not many Western tourists, mostly Thai young professionals, Japanese tourists/ expats and a few young professional Western expats here and there.

- **Phrom Phong:** Location of 2 of Bangkok's classiest malls (Emporium and EmQuartier) and Benjasiri Park. Many Asian tourists and Thai high society types.

- **Asok:** Area near Asok Road and BTS Station, home to popular Terminal 21 shopping mall, Benchakiti Park, and the highest concentration of upscale hotels on Sukhumvit. Very heavy Western foreigner presence and Western-style establishments, but not even remotely close to feeling like the West.

- **Nana:** Mainly an entertainment/ nightlife area, with seedier nightlife on Soi 4 and (more) upscale nightlife on Soi 11. Mostly a mix of Western, Arabic and Indian expats, tourists and restaurants, and some Thai nightclub goers. Soi 11 is popular for upscale dining, bars, nightclubs, and a few famous rooftop bars.

Where to Stay: I recommend first-time visitors to stay around **Asok**. The area is right on the BTS, in the middle of major malls, spas, restaurants, and nightlife, and there are hundreds of hotels. Plus, every other area of Bangkok you need to see is a quick trip from here.

Silom

The **Silom** area, just Southwest of Sukhumvit, is Bangkok's Central Business District. A mix of Western and Asian tourists both come for the cheap souvenir shopping at the Patpong night market and the wild nightlife the area is also famous for within the same few blocks. Lumphini Stadium holds regular Muay Thai fights, and Lumphini Park is a great daytime spot for exercise or people watching. Serviced by both BTS and MRT via the Sala Daeng and Lumphini stops, respectively.

Where to Stay: Stay near the Sala Daeng BTS station. Quick access to the BTS which links to the Sukhumvit line in 2 stops, and also the dining, nightlife and Lumphini Park makes it a great location.

Siam

Technically still on Sukhumvit Road, the **Siam** area is most notable for its giant malls: Siam Paragon (high-end), Central World and Siam Square (middle tier), and MBK (mostly clothing market, lower tier). Also home to the many boutique shops, cafes, the Hard Rock Café, Jim Thompson House and a few other notable spots. Not much in the way of hotels or nightlife.

Where to Stay: Unless you came to shop at the Siam malls, don't stay around Siam. If you did, stay near the Siam BTS.

Pratunam

Just North of Siam is Pratunam, another major shopping destination best known for Pantip Plaza, a huge electronics mall, and its many surrounding markets. Host to a number of upscale hotels, but not so much nightlife. Great access to the water taxis and walkable to the Siam area, but no BTS.

Where to Stay: Due to lack of major restaurants and nightlife, I would not recommend staying in Pratunam, unless that's what you're seeking. Also, it's problematic getting in or out during bad traffic times due to lack of a BTS station. It is, however, serviced by the water taxis.

Khaosan Road (Banglampu Neighborhood)

Nestled on the East side of the Chayapraya River, and not far from the temples and Grand Palace, **Khaosan Road** is generally known as the home to the young (and old) Western backpacking community. A mix of Western and Asian tourists, the area is worth a visit even if you don't plan on resting your head here. The rooms are affordable (though stay off of Khaosan itself if you don't like noise) as is everything else around here. The atmosphere is very fun, with live music and cheap drinks flowing well into the morning; however, very touristy and in the heart of Tuk Tuk town (meaning that the Tuk Tuk traps are probably going to be your only way in or out).

Where to Stay: If you need to actually sleep, stay in one of the side streets, not actually on Khaosan. Also, unless you plan to spend most of your time in Old Bangkok, I wouldn't stay around there long due to the issues with getting in and out via the overpriced Tuk Tuks.

Riverside (Thonburi Neighborhood)

Just South/ Southwest of Khaosan, you can find quite a few hotels (little pricier, this is where most of the 5 start hotels are) right on the East bank of the river, many with great sunset views of Wat Arun (Temple of the Dawn), the Grand Palace, and everything else in this historic area. It gets pretty quiet after dark, which can be relaxing. There are a few markets around, small cafes and restaurants, and oh yeah, also in Tuk Tuk town, though closer to the BTS than Khaosan Road. For a *really* great view of the sun setting behind Wat Arun, have a few drinks at the Eagle Nest Bar. More hotel offerings line the East bank of the river further South, mostly 5-star rated.

Where to Stay: With the best views in Bangkok, you can't go wrong here. The Hilton, Oriental, and Sheraton are located here.

Petchaburi Road

Running parallel and just north of Sukhumvit, and worth a mention only because of the RCA entertainment district. RCA is a large collection of restaurants and nightclubs visited by young professional Thais and expats, with a lack of seediness and panhandling that permeates many of the other popular areas in the city. Recommended for nightlife only.

Where to Stay: I don't recommend staying on Petchaburi Road due to lack of anything very interesting.

Chinatown

Bangkok has the oldest, and largest, **Chinatown** in the world. Chinatown is host to a few upscale hotels, not known for any particular nightlife, and is best known, amongst Thais and visitors, for the amazing variety of street food on offer. If you're a foodie, you need to go here. Just West of Hua Lamphong station, South of the Riverside area, around Yaowarat Road.

Where to Stay: I do not recommend staying in Chinatown, due to the area shutting down around 11:00 pm, and the lack of a nearby BTS station.

For a thorough breakdown of these areas and more, based on proximity to transport, attractions and accommodations, visit 40MinuteTravelGuru.com.

Nightlife

"Bangkok, like Las Vegas, sounds like a place where you make bad

decisions."

-Todd Phillips, on the filming of The Hangover II

While it's very true that the Asian "City of Angels" can take you down some pretty dark rabbit holes if you allow it, it's also a whole lot of fun to see where they go. I mean the *epic* type of fun. Whatever your version of a great night on the town is, you'll find it, and many things you didn't even know could be found, during a few nights out in Bangkok (or even 1 night as the song suggests). The below activities and places should get you quickly heading in the right direction:

- **Sukhumvit Soi 11:** Nightclubs, Western-style bars, and pubs, Above Eleven rooftop bar. The street is always partying, every day of the week, and it's never too early. Western expats, tourists, and Thais.

- **Rooftop Bars:** Bangkok is world famous for the stunning nighttime views of the city some of the rooftop bars have to offer. Cocktail sipping at rooftop bars in Bangkok while the sun sets and the city turns on its lights, transforming into the nocturnal animal that it is, is something you can't miss. Get a good table by reserving in advance as this has become a favorite pastime of visitors.

- **Nana:** Nana Plaza (on Sukhumvit Soi 4) and the surrounding area is known for its seedy entertainment, but there are some otherwise decent live music venues and bars here as well. Again, it doesn't have to be "night" here for nightlife either. Frequented by mostly Western foreigners.

- **Phra Kanong/ W Market:** A short walk East from the BTS. Relax for some outdoor food and drinks at the W Market before heading out for your night. Lots of small food stalls and interior outdoor seating. Favorite amongst the Thais and Western expat crowd.

- **Ratchada Rot Fai Train Market:** Mostly Thais and Asian tourists, a huge outdoor street food market, with some very cool shops and restaurants. You can walk around, select your food, find a table and be served your drinks by the staff. The place to go to eat and drink like the locals and save some money.

- **Silom:** As mentioned, home to the Patpong Night Market, but also a big nightlife area. Frequented by Western and Asian visitors for the nightlife.

- **Khaosan Road:** Steady mix of a wide variety of foreign visitors and Thais, partying until the morning in the nightclubs, pubs and in the street.

- **RCA:** Mostly Thai young professional crowd. A few really large nightclubs here, and doesn't get started until after midnight.

Attractions

If you're short on time, make sure to do these *AT A MINIMUM* to get a real sense of the city and culture:

- Visit the Temples at the **Grand Palace, Wat Arun,** and **Wat Pho**;

- Sip cocktails at **Moon Bar, Above Eleven** or **Skybar**;

- Eat street food in **Chinatown**;

- See a Muay Thai match at **Rajadamnern Stadium** or **Lumphini Boxing Stadium**.

- Go souvenir shopping at **Chatuchak** weekend market, or **Patpong** night market.

Phuket

Phuket is perhaps the most popular beachside destination for most foreign travelers to Thailand. A big (bigger than many think) island in the South, nestled on the beautiful Andaman Sea and about an hour flight from Bangkok, Phuket has all of the things your likely to expect in Thailand: Beaches, spicy food, elephants, tigers, temples, more beaches, raucous nightlife, and Muay Thai can all be found here.

Getting There

Phuket is accessible via either of the main airports in Bangkok with numerous daily flights, as well as many direct international flights. In addition to air travel, Phuket can be reached from Bangkok, as well as Malaysia, via rail and bus.

Getting Around

Taxis, Grab/ Uber and motorbikes will be your primary means of transport around the island, as no train system operates. If you are an experienced rider, it may make sense to rent a motorbike here, as getting from town to town via the taxis and Tuk Tuk mafia will quickly start to lighten your wallet. For these reasons, it's better to stay close to where you plan to spend most of your time or rotate the area you stay in to match your desired activities.

Where to Stay

Phuket has roughly 5 main towns to choose from, each one having its own attractions, pros and cons of course. Outside of these main towns, there are other options as well that you could explore on your own.

Patong: Known as the wild party town, Patong has a decent (but not great) beach, *MANY* bars, many restaurants, and a wild nightlife scene. Not even close to a family friendly place, and even as a young single traveler the chaos might begin to wear on you after a few days if you require some real rest and relaxation. If Patpong in Bangkok had a beach, it would surely be Patong.

Karon: 20-minutes South of Patong, Karon offers a nicer beach, with a toned-down party environment. Better if you want to rest, enjoy the beach and avoid the raunchiness, crowds, and noise. Karon is certainly a happy medium, and not too far from Patong if you feel like venturing there.

Kamala: 20-minutes north of Patong, Kamala has a great beach, restaurants and beach bars but not much in the way of nightlife. More relaxing than the other mentioned areas, so perhaps a good choice if you're planning to remain fairly sedentary. If not, perhaps Karon is a better location.

Phuket Town: Not a beachside town, but good proximity to many choices due to its location in the center of the island. Perhaps a good choice if you want to be well located to venture around to other sites during the day. A little bit of nightlife can be found, but not much.

Nightlife

As if it wasn't clear yet, Phuket's only real nightlife to speak of is in, yes, Patong. If you're staying here, it will be apparent. The center of the nightlife scene in Patong is on Bangla Road. Here you'll find bars, pubs, nightclubs and plenty of the risqué entertainment the area is famous for. Partying goes on all night, year-round.

Attractions

Besides the many beaches on the island, Phuket has no shortage of must-see sites and must-do activities. Here are the most popular:

Phang Nga Bay: Home to James Bond Island (the tall island in the center of the bay), named so for the filming of a Bond film here, one of the most frequented bays and beaches around.

Ko Phi Phi: Famous for its role in the movie *The Beach*. Shut down in 2018 due to over tourism, but a beautiful place. Recommend visiting in the offseason to avoid crowds.

Bangla Road: The wild street is worth checking out, even if you aren't the partying type.

Bangla Boxing Stadium: Muay Thai fights are held year-round here, with a mix of Thai and foreign fighters.

Big Buddha: 120-foot tall white Buddha at the top of a hill overlooking Phuket. Great views from the top and you can elephant trek on your way up.

Elephant Trekking: Phuket has a few different Elephant operators on the island.

Similan Islands: Some of the most beautiful islands in Thailand, the natural park consists of numerous small islands, accessible from Phuket via ferry. Some of the best diving in the world can be found here.

Hua Hin

One of the few beachside getaways close to Bangkok, **Hua Hin** is also the historical vacation home of the royal family. More popular with Thais than tourists, the beaches aren't nearly as scenic as Krabi or Phuket, and there's not much nightlife, but it can make for a nice trip if you need a few days to get away from the smoke and traffic of Bangkok.

Getting There

Located Southwest of Bangkok, on the West side of the Gulf of Thailand, Hua Hin can be reached via train (4 hours), bus (3 hours) or car (2 hours).

Where to Stay

Hua Hin has a main road running North to South through the middle of it, with many beachfront accommodations available on the East side. I recommend staying near or just south of the city center, as the beaches are not bad here, and this is where you'll find the restaurants and little nightlife. If you desire a more remote and less touristy beach, stay a bit North in Cha-Am.

Nightlife and Attractions

Both Hua Hin and Cha-Am are modeled around family beach vacations for Thais. So, the majority of people come here to eat, drink and stay around the beach. With that said, there are a few things to do other than that:

Cicada Market: Night market and beer garden with live music in Cha-Am.

Soi Bintabat: The only nightlife in Hua Hin would be found on and around Soi Bintabat.

Hilton Sky Bar: The only sky bar in Hua Hin.

Hua Hin Night Market: Typical Thai night market at the city center every night of the week.

Khao Takiab: Temple situated atop a beachside hill at the southern end of Hua Hin. Great views and relaxing beachside bars in this area.

Chiang Mai

Thailand's 2nd largest city, and unofficial capital of the North, Chiang Mai is a stark contrast with the densely populated Bangkok and the clear water beaches along the Andaman Sea in the South. Most notable for its mountains and temples, Chiang Mai is also a bustling nightlife destination and home to many digital nomads seeking an escape from the higher costs of the more touristy areas in the South.

Getting There

Daily flights are offered from either of Bangkok's main airports. Additionally, the State Railway of Thailand offers overnight sleeper trains, and standard trains, direct from Hua Lamphong Station in Bangkok.

Getting Around

Like everywhere else outside of Bangkok, taxis and motorbikes will be your mode of transport. Additionally, Songthaews are very common in Chiang Mai and each one has a route provided in English. This is a much cheaper alternative to taxis, but not as exciting as a motorbike.

Where to Stay

Chiang Mai has a few different areas worth staying in. A big city, but certainly not Bangkok, you could easily choose where to stay based on your preference for sleep and get around the entire city during the day without much trouble.

Riverside: Very laid-back area with street vendors, markets, and affordable hotels. The nightlife consists of open-air beer gardens, night markets, and Thai style music venues. Not fancy, not in your face and not too lively.

Old City: Literally, the walls around this area used to contain Chiang Mai, now it simply contains some of the older parts of the city. This includes the majority of the temples that Chiang Mai is famous for. There are a few night markets and a bit of nightlife, but nothing too trendy or lively.

Nimman Road: The trendy and liveliest section of the city, notable for its cafes, nightclubs, and shopping. If you desire to stay in a boutique hotel and sip cocktails at a rooftop bar, this is probably where you should stay.

Nightlife and Attractions

As far as nightlife goes, each of the main areas of the city has its own nightlife atmosphere, and each area is easily accessed from other areas, so you should feel free to stay in one area and frequent other areas for the nightlife.

As far as attractions, Chiang Mai has plenty to do during the day:

See the Temples: The Old City is full of Chiang Mai's oldest temples, drawing many of the visitors in the first place. Outside of those, Wat Doi Suthep and Wat Suan Dok and Wat Umong should be on your list.

Market Hopping: The Night Bazaar, Sunday Walking Street, Waulai Walking Street, and Warorat Market are the best markets to visit in Chiang Mai.

Visit an Elephant Sanctuary: More than a few sanctuaries exist around Chiang Mai where you'll be allowed to feed and interact with Elephants, adults, and babies. A few Elephant trekking operations exist as well.

Pattaya and Jomtien

Pattaya, commonly referred to as Sin City Thailand, is the physical manifestation of every seedy and negative stereotype of Thailand that every foreigner is unfortunately familiar with. Home to literally thousands of bars, the city is one giant entertainment district (the word cesspool does come to mind), with almost every local engaged in some way, shape or form, with the raunchy nightlife economy. In no way a good representation of the rest of Thailand, this city is really only good for wild nightlife. If you're seeking a beach getaway, you're on the wrong side of the Gulf. If you're seeking a wild time, you'll surely find it here.

Jomtien, however, is much more relaxed, with a much cleaner beach (Pattaya Beach is notoriously filthy) and less in-your-face raunchiness. About 15 minutes South by taxi,

Getting There

Daily buses depart Bangkok for the 2 to 3-hour trip, with taxis and private cars costing around 2,000 Baht.

Getting Around

Most people tend to stay on or around the beach, making transportation easy. Songthaews and motorcycle taxis will be your only method of reasonable transport around the city. If you choose to stay further out of town, or in nearby Jomtien Beach, regular taxis or Grab taxis will be a better option.

Where to Stay

Many hotels, and Airbnb's, due to the current condo boom, are available on or near the beach. In Pattaya, I would recommend staying in Central or Southern Pattaya for access to Beach Road and Walking Street, the two tourist areas. For Jomtien, most accommodations are located right on Beach Road.

Nightlife and Attractions

We've already established the infamously wild nightlife on hand in Pattaya. In addition to that, there are a few other notable things to do.

Walking Street: After dark, Walking Street in Pattaya is more comparable to a circus than any other "Walking Street" you'll find in Asia. Not a market in sight, hundreds of adult bars, nightclubs and live music venues line the street, which is closed to traffic and crowded with every type of personality, both good and bad, but mostly not the church-going type, from everywhere in the world.

Siracha Tiger Zoo: About 30 minutes North, the Siracha Tiger Zoo (located in the town of Siracha) houses a very large Tiger population, as well as Crocodiles. The money maker here is the Tiger circus, photos with Tigers (both adults and babies) and Crocodile feeding.

Koh Lan: A very scenic island accessible by boat, Koh Larn is more in line with the mental image most have of Thailand: White sand beaches and clear water. Good for a day trip, and there are some great accommodations on the island.

Rayong: Not in Pattaya or Jomtien, but a 2-hour ride South. The beaches of Rayong are straight out of a Thai travel brochure, and with significantly less foreign tourists than Pattaya or Jomtien.

Songkran: Not a location, but the traditional Thai New Year is celebrated in Pattaya in April of each year. This is a highly recommended time to visit if that's your cup of tea, as the city erupts into a celebration comparable to Mardi Gras or Carnival in Brazil for 3 or 4 days. Also celebrated across the country, but on a much larger scale in Pattaya.

Koh Samui

Nestled on the Western side of the Gulf of Thailand, **Koh Samui** is the essence of Thailand's reputation as a beach getaway destination. Lacking the raunchy nightlife of Patong or Pattaya, the beaches in Koh Samui are crystal clear, and getting beach Thai massages all day is the favorite pastime of most visitors.

Getting There and Getting Around

Daily flights from both airports in Bangkok are your only option. Koh Samui IS an island. While on the island, renting a motorbike is a safe bet, or there are plenty of Tuk Tuks and taxis. Going rules apply.

Where to Stay

Koh Samui can be broken up into main areas, each with its own beaches and nightlife.

Chaweng Beach: The most popular, nicest and busiest beach, this is where the majority of visitors sleep, eat and play. Plenty of beach bars, restaurants and nightclubs, and plenty of company too.

Lamai Beach: Milder atmosphere than Chaweng during the day, but stunning beaches and plenty to keep you well fed and shopped. The nightlife gets a bit wild, but nothing like Patong.

Maenam Beach: The resident backpacker beach, this is where you can find the low-cost beach bungalow of your dreams.

Bo Phut Beach: Laid back, with plenty of watersports on hand.

Nightlife and Attractions

The majority of nightlife can be found on Chaweng and Lamai Beaches after dark, but you'll never be completely without it anywhere on the island. During the day, beyond your typical beach activities of getting sunburned and massaged, there are a few things you can do.

Koh Phangan: Adjacent to Koh Samui, Koh Phangan is most known for its wild Full Moon parties and its diving community, being one of the best dive locations in Thailand. The smaller island also hosts a wild nightlife scene of its own, any night of the week.

Koh Tao: One of the other beautiful islands around Koh Samui.

Namuang Waterfall: Picturesque waterfalls.

Mummified Monks: Koh Samui is home to a few mummified monks, on display, whose dying wishes were to be mummified. Creepy, but I bet you'll want to see it if you go.

Snorkeling and Diving: As stated, this area is host to some of the best in Thailand. Koh Tao, Koh Phangan, and the Angthong Marine Park are all once in a lifetime diving opportunities. Dive operations are plentiful.

Isaan (Northeastern Thailand)

Certainly not in many Thailand travel brochures, the giant Northern countryside region of Isaan is where a large majority of the Thais you'll meet working in the tourism sector across the country come from. Very rural, but with a few major cities, think of Isaan as the Midwestern United States of Thailand. The people of Isaan share the same Khmer heritage with that of neighboring Cambodia and Laos, and many speak the same dialect. As Thailand's "country folk" they are what you'd expect: Exceptional cooks and incredibly friendly.

The Isaan food, music, and culture all have its own distinct character. The food is a bit spicier, and not commonly found in your typical Thai restaurant in your home country. Avoid raw fish, as it's been known to contain liver flukes. Also, fried insects are considered a treat here, and commonly eaten as a snack, as are frogs.

A good night out will consist of a large meal of many different dishes out at an outdoor market, served with plenty of drinks. Expect to be served iced beer, as it's the only way to enjoy a beer in Isaan, all while listening to live Isaan music, which is very upbeat and fun to get into. The Isaan Thais are a really good time.

I do recommend a visit through Isaan if you have the time, also great to explore on your way to Cambodia or Laos if that's on your agenda. As mentioned before, the Koh Samui's and Phuket's of the country are great, but that's really all a façade to keep the tourist dollars flowing. If you want to experience the *real* Thailand, hop a train or bus through Isaan. If you plan to travel to a specific city in Isaan, direct flights to the major cities run from Don Mueang Airport in Bangkok, but both bus and railway service are much cheaper if you're up for that experience.

Honorable Mention

There are clearly more regions to visit in Thailand, but going into great detail for each is outside the scope of this book. For more detailed information with plenty of links, maps, and local recommendations, I urge you to visit my Thailand page at 40MinuteTravelGuru.com.

Ayutthaya

The ancient capital of Siam, great for a quick day trip from Bangkok to check out the ruins. Plan on at least a half-day. Book through a tour operator or ask any taxi driver as many will agree and are also familiar with the temples you'll want to see.

Kanchanaburi

Should be on any World War II history buff's agenda, the location of the famous *Bridge Over the River Kwai* along the Death Railway to Myanmar (Burma), built by allied POW's during the Japanese occupation of Thailand. Railway tours are a popular trip for many.

Chiang Rai

Nestled in the Northwest corner near Myanmar, Laos and not far from Chiang Mai, Chiang Rai is a great place for temple sightseeing and is also home to some of the famous hill tribes of Thailand, known for the gold rings they wear around their elongated necks from childhood.

Krabi

The mainland province just East of Phuket is home to hundreds of the tall limestone cliffs this area is known for, as well as many low-key beaches more beautiful and less populated than the ones in neighboring Phuket. Krabi is overall a more relaxing time, with little nightlife when compared to Phuket.

Koh Chang

Located off the coast of Eastern Thailand close to Cambodia, Koh Chang is also home to amazing beaches, and since it's harder to get to, has fewer visitors, and less nightlife. Very great place to relax.

Koh Samet

Just off the coast of Rayong and 4 hours from Bangkok, another great out of the way location for amazing scenery.

Koh Lipe

Quite a distance off the Southern coast, almost to Malaysia, Koh Lipe is another island hosting pristine beaches that may be able to provide some genuine rest away from the hoards. Expect a journey with plenty of trains, buses, and ferries getting there.

Koh Lanta

Island just south of Krabi, and East of Koh Phi Phi.

Koh Lak

2 hours north of Phuket by bus, Koh Lak is home to pristine beaches with a direct Westerly view of the Andaman Sea.

For additional articles containing reviews, recommendations, tips and tricks for other countries you plan on visiting, browse the wealth of travel tips and information available at 40MinuteTravelGuru.com.

CPSIA information can be obtained
at www.ICGtesting.com
Printed in the USA
FSHW012120161219
65173FS